Dinah Zike's
Notebook Foldables®
for Binders, Spirals, and Composition Books

Strategies for All Subjects
Grades 4 - College

Dinah-Might Adventures, LP
P.O. Box 690328
San Antonio, Texas, 78269
Phone (210) 698-0123
Fax (210) 698-0095
ORDERS ONLY: 1-800-99-DINAH
Visit our website www.dinah.com

Copyright © 2008 Dinah Zike
3rd Edition 2011
Published by Dinah-Might Adventures, LP, San Antonio, Texas
www.dinah.com 1-800-99DINAH

ISBN-13: 978-1-882796-27-4
ISBN-10: 1-882796-27-6

Editors
Jan Manzanero, Dr. Rhonda Meyer, Ignacio Salas-Humara, Dr. Judi Youngers
Book Design and Layout
Dinah Zike and Ignacio Salas-Humara
Photography
Ignacio Salas-Humara
All photos copyright © 2008 Dinah-Might Adventures, LP

Dedication

I dedicate this book to the thousands of educators who helped me battle cancer through their e-mails, cards, shared experiences, thoughts and prayers. To those I know personally, and to those I haven't met who reached out to me in a spirit of goodwill, I send my warmest gratitude and best wishes.

Thank You!

A special thank-you to teachers who have attended the Dinah Zike Academy for your feedback and suggestions on Notebook Foldables®. We hope your enthusiasm and love for Notebook Foldables® will be shared by teachers everywhere.

The words and pictures from *real world print* (RWP) used in the photographed examples in this book came from numerous newspapers, magazines, flyers, and advertisements from across the U.S. -- all valuable teaching tools. The vast majority of the words and phrases used on the Foldables® and VKVs™ were found in the following publications, or supplements to these publications:
USA Today, San Antonio Express-News, Austin American-Statesman.

Dinah Zike's
Notebook Foldables®

for Binders, Spirals, and Composition Books

Strategies for all Subjects
Grades 4 - College

Copyright © 2008, Dinah Zike
Dinah-Might Adventures, LP
San Antonio, Texas
www.dinah.com

Please contact DMA for permission
to use parts of this book in
workshops, classes, or presentations:
(210) 698-0123 or dma@dinah.com

Table of Contents

Welcome to Dinah's latest -- Notebook Foldables!

Notebook Foldables work well in any subject area to stimulate ideas and represent information in a format more familiar and useful to more advanced/upper level students. These are adaptations of Dinah's Foldables specially designed to fit in composition books, spiral notebooks, binders, and even exam books. You'll be amazed at how many examples you see in these pages, and we hope they prompt you to think of even more variations.

While any Foldable helps students organize complicated information, Notebook Foldables offer an opportunity for teacher-directed or student-directed color coding of information via the double border area surrounding the Notebook Foldable. Teachers might ask students to color-code information according to that which will be covered on an exam, or related to specific headings in the text. Alternately, students might leave the double borders blank until they feel they've mastered it, and color code it according to subject area or chapter headings.

Also, while Dinah developed these adaptations specifically for the materials students use on a daily basis in the classroom, these templates could also be enlarged and used to create interactive posters, bulletin boards or portable display boards, like those used at science fairs.

As you know, at Dinah Might Adventures, LP, we strive to provide you materials that can be used as flexibly as you need them to. On these pages, you'll find templates that you can adapt to your needs. If you don't need all of them, don't use all of them; if you need to make a modification, make that modification. Our goal is to help you maximize the resources at your disposal so that you can teach at your highest level and your students can learn as much as possible in their time with you.

These Notebook Foldables are an exciting development for us—this product is not specific to one subject area but works across subject areas. For those of you who would like to get suggestions for specific topics, Dinah has included ideas for using this book in conjunction with her Big Book series. Those of you who are looking for a way to maximize the composition books, spirals, and binders already in use in your classroom, enjoy!

Rhonda Meyer
Chief Operating Officer
Dinah-Might Adventures, LP

How to Use Regular Paper to Make Notebook Foldables:

1. FOLD
an anchor tab and the desired number of information tabs.

2. GLUE
the anchor tab.

3. CUT
information tabs.

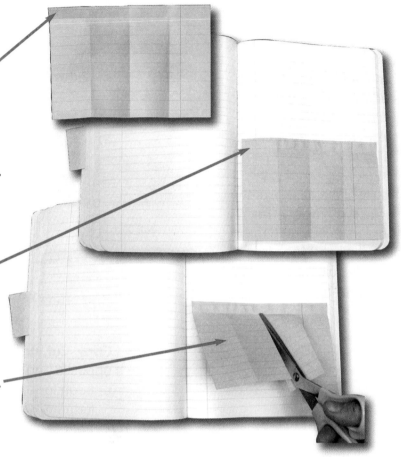

Color Outside the Lines: Color tabs or trace along outline borders before cutting out Notebook Foldables. Notebook Foldables are not art projects, and valuable class time cannot be wasted on excessive coloring.

Color Code Borders: The double-line borders around the Notebook Foldable Templates can be used to organize student work or differentiate between activities. Borders might be color-coded to indicate the objective being studied, work completed within a given chapter, the level of difficulty of the activity, or the degree of objective mastery. For example, borders not colored might indicate that information needs to be learned, while colored borders indicate that information has been mastered.

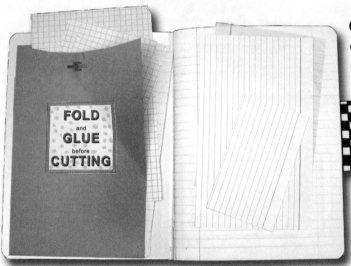

Copy, Cut, and Paste: The signs on the opposite page can be duplicated to make enough for every student to have one. (Left) The reminder was glued onto the front of an 6" x 9 " envelope that was cut to form a two-sided pocket and used in the front of a composition book for storage. See pages 29-31 for more information on the placement of envelopes within notebooks.

FOLD
and
GLUE
before
CUTTING

FOLD
and
GLUE
before
CUTTING

FOLD
and
GLUE
before
CUTTING

FOLD
and
GLUE
before
CUTTING

FOLD
and
GLUE
before
CUTTING

FOLD
and
GLUE
before
CUTTING

Dear Friends and Educators,

I am frequently asked, "When did you invent *Foldables*?" and "How did you become the 'hamburger' and 'hotdog' lady?" It is a story that I enjoy sharing with teachers and students, and I'd like to share it with you to provide a historic reference for the 3-D instructional strategies presented in this book.

I first started designing and using paper-based manipulatives when I was in sixth grade. I used them as study aids to help organize my own notes in junior high, and later in high school and college, and I discovered they also worked as study aids for students I tutored throughout high school. Later, to earn money for college, I worked with students with severe learning disabilities. I continued to design paper-based study aids, or manipulatives, and invented names for the folds I used to make the manipulatives. Hamburger, hotdog, taco, burrito, and shutterfold were some of my first terms because they were easy for my "students" to remember. I adopted, or borrowed, the terms mountain and valley from origami books and programs.

Sometimes I got ideas for new manipulatives from greeting card folds or folded advertisements; but most of the time, I would just take paper and fold it to illustrate something I needed to remember or something I needed to teach others. This was the beginning of *Foldables*, even though they were not called that at the time, and when I tell you I started Junior High School in 1966 and graduated from high school in 1970, you will be able to do the math -- I've been designing, using, and teaching others to use my three-dimensional graphic organizers for over 40 years.

After graduating from college, I became a teacher. I taught school during the week and presented workshops and continuing education sessions for schools and conferences on the weekends. With the help of excited, creative teachers who attended my presentations, my three-dimensional graphic organizers began to spread across the U.S. I remember, too, how thrilling it was to receive my first letters from teachers who were using my manipulatives in other countries.

In the 1970's and early 1980's, my folds and manipulatives were met with resounding approval in my teacher workshops, but when I presented my ideas for 3-D manipulatives to major publishing companies, I met rejection. I was told that the strategies were too time consuming, too dependent upon student production and writing, too artsy-craftsy for upper level students, and innumerable other negative critiques. For several years I tried to find a publisher who would print books containing instructions on how to make and use my three-dimensional graphic organizers. You have to remember, this was thirty-five years ago, and the world of education was paper based; but the paper was used to produce "ditto sheets" or duplicated worksheets, not 3-D study aids. To put this time in perspective, know that it was before most of the brain research was published, before cooperative learning was an accepted practice, and years before two-dimensional graphic organizers began to appear in nearly every educational publication -- supplemental and required -- as duplicable sheets. And, the duplicated worksheets we used at that time were made on a crank machine that used a powerful fluid to copy information imbedded on purple masters.

Completely frustrated, and with a file drawer full of rejections, I withdrew all the money I had accrued in my teacher retirement fund, and with a loan from my local bank, I began my own publishing company in my garage in 1984. My first publications were not based upon my folds, even though I was still inventing new folds and using both the old and new manipulatives in my classroom, in my graduate work, and in my staff development training sessions. My company had to make money to succeed, so I began by publishing the thematic units I used in my classroom and taught in my staff development sessions. I also published social studies materials I had developed to teach the history of my state of Texas. I knew these were teaching aids that were needed and easily understood, and they would generate the revenue I needed to publish my book of 3-D manipulatives. (Reflecting back, I think I lacked the self-confidence to put what little money I had into a book based solely on my folds because my folding activities had received rejections from so many very successful companies!)

In 1986, after two years of garage publishing, I wrote my first book consisting entirely of my folds and 3-D graphic organizers. It was entitled *Dinah Zike's Big Book of Books and Activities*, and, like my other self-published books, it consisted of photocopied pages bound with notebook rings or brads. I often gave away parts of it as a handout at my workshops. In 1991, my company published the official, bound version of this award-winning book and included black-line illustrations to accompany the fold instructions, along with black-and-white photographs. It was one of the first, if not the first, supplemental educational book to use more photographs than black-line art.

Over the years I continued to design, publish, and teach others using my three-dimensional graphic organizers, and they continued to gain popularity as teachers who used them successfully shared them with others. My folds were spreading across the country, and it was rewarding to see my ideas and hear my terms used by students, teachers, and professors. When I presented the Mary C. McCurdy lecture at the National Science Teacher's Conference in 2000, Glencoe McGraw-Hill approached me to include my 3-D graphic organizers in their textbooks. Michael Oster, my dear friend with McGraw-Hill, coined the term *Foldables*® for my 3-D graphic organizers, and today my *Foldables*® are an exclusive feature of McGraw-Hill School Solutions. They appear as a study aid in nearly every K-12 McGraw-Hill textbook and many McGraw-Hill ancillaries.

Two-dimensional graphic organizers have been in use for decades, and I am certainly not the first person to fold paper to teach a skill or concept; but I started and popularized the practice of using innumerable three-dimensional graphic organizers as teaching aids and developing them into a supplemental program based upon proven, research-based skills and strategies. When I take Venn diagrams, concept maps, KWL lists, comparing and contrasting activities, and other research-based graphic organizers and make them into *Foldables*®, they have tabs or layers so main ideas can be written and viewed clearly on the top plane and supporting facts, definitions, and notes can be recorded on underlying planes -- or under the tabs. (See Research Citations, pages 116 to 118.)

You will see my *Foldables*® used in other people's presentations and publications, and most give credit to the source; but as the originator of *Foldables*® and VKVs™ (Visual Kinesthetic Vocabulary manipulatives), I present this <u>notebook-dependent</u> <u>variation</u> of *Foldables* as an extension of my <u>independent</u> <u>3-D</u> <u>graphic</u> <u>organizers</u>. Please use my many content-specific *Foldable*® publications to find hundreds of ideas on ways you can use Notebook *Foldables*® and VKVs™ (Visual Kinesthetic Vocabulary Flashcards) with grades 4-college.

Have fun and be creative as you use and adapt the *Foldables* in this book!

Dinah Zike, M.Ed.

Before

During

After

With Husband, Ignacio Salas-Humara

Please support breast cancer research and awareness programs.
Tell those you love to get mammograms.

Ideas for Content-Specific Foldables®

I am frequently asked, "How do I get ideas for Foldables?" Over a fifteen-year period, I collected lists of examples of ways Foldables could be used in the content areas of math, science, and social sciences. Compilations of these lists are featured in my *Big Book* series. The book titles are listed at the bottom of this page.

Photograph from the front section of Dinah Zike's *Big Book of Math*.

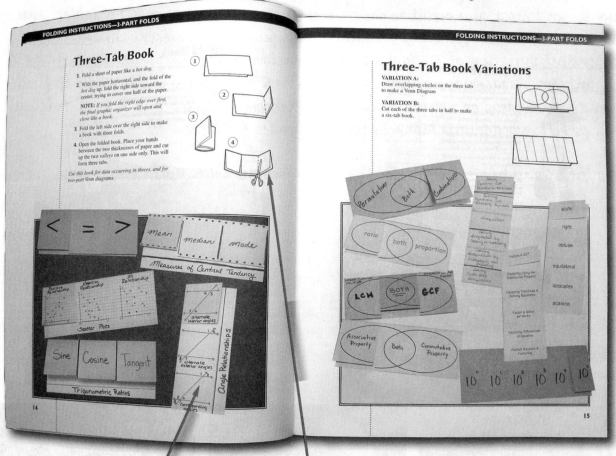

The front section of each of the books in the *Big Book* series has written instructions and diagrams to illustrate the steps for making Foldables, and color photographs of sample Foldables that have been made. The Foldables photographed are content specific to each book, thus examples differ for each book. The instructions are organized by the number of tabs or sections created by the Foldable. As seen in the third column of the lists illustrated on the next page, the number helps teachers and/or students find an appropriate Foldable to kinesthetically represent a skill or concept studied.

The following Dinah Zike Foldables books are available at www.dinah.com:

...*Big Book of Elementary Math*
...*Big Book of Middle School/High School Math*
...*Big Book of Elementary Science*
...*Big Book of Middle School/High School Science*
...*Big Book of Elementary Social Studies*
...*Big Book of United States History*
...*Big Book of World History*
...*Big Book of Texas History*

All of the Foldable activities featured in this series of content-specific books can be used with Notebook Foldables. Look to the *Big Books* for Foldable ideas to be used with the templates featured in this book and on the accompanying CD.

Photograph from the extensive list section of Dinah Zike's ***Big Book of World History***.

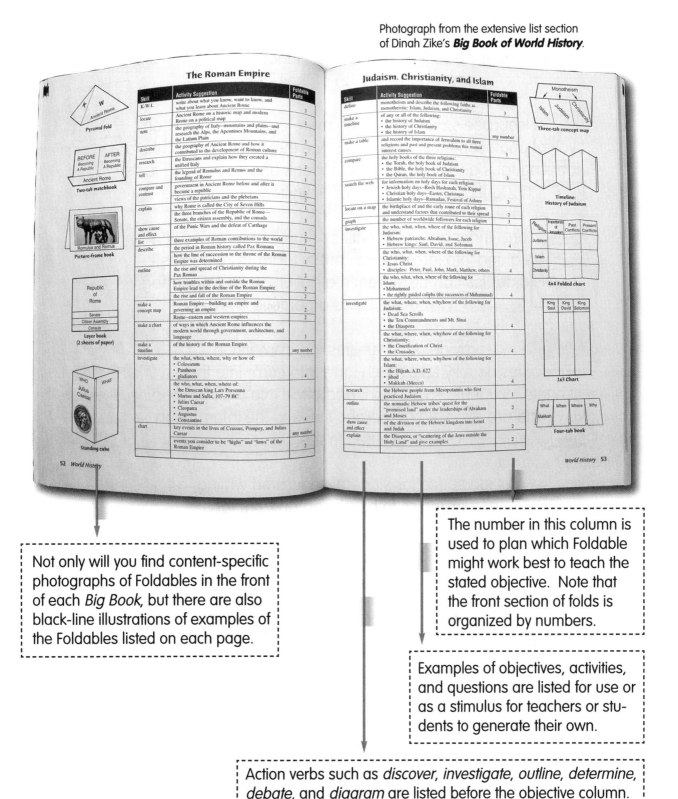

Not only will you find content-specific photographs of Foldables in the front of each *Big Book,* but there are also black-line illustrations of examples of the Foldables listed on each page.

The number in this column is used to plan which Foldable might work best to teach the stated objective. Note that the front section of folds is organized by numbers.

Examples of objectives, activities, and questions are listed for use or as a stimulus for teachers or students to generate their own.

Action verbs such as *discover, investigate, outline, determine, debate,* and *diagram* are listed before the objective column.

Dinah Zike's
Independent Foldables®...

...use one or more sheets of paper to form
independent student work or projects that students can store ⟵
easily and work on at their desks.

...encourage students to write more than they would on
typical photocopied worksheets since they are responsible for ⟵
labeling tabs and recording main ideas and supporting facts,
thoughts, questions, terms, definitions, and more.

...form independent activities. Smaller Foldables can
be glued into larger-sized, project-format Foldables. ⟵
All Foldables can be stored in a gallon-sized zipper bag
which serves as a portfolio.

...provide opportunities for "immersion."
Foldables usually take much longer to complete than work- ⟵
sheets. Students invest work and effort into their production
and are exposed numerous times to the information
presented in them.

...provide space for student-generated writing, art,
and graphics to be placed on front tabs ⟵
as well as under the tabs.

...turn note-taking, study guides, and projects
into tangible objects which students regard with pride and ⟵
view as learning accomplishments.

Dinah Zike's
Notebook Foldables®...

...use sections of paper that are **dependent** upon a sheet of paper within a binder, spiral, or composition book to form the back of the Foldable.

...increase the amount of writing space within a notebook by adding another dimension to pages while providing all the advantages of independent Foldables.

...allow students to take notes within the same notebook into which they glue their Foldables and VKVs (Visual Kinesthetic Vocabulary), resulting in a compilation of multiple activities that forms a comprehensive study guide.

...like Independent Foldables, provide opportunities for "immersion," since they are a collection of student work produced over a period of weeks or months. Students usually use several notebooks during a school term.

...provide space for student-generated writing, art, and graphics. Or computer-generated templates can be used for art, graphics, and text to be generated by the teacher or students electronically.

...result in note-taking, study guides, and projects in which students take pride. As notebooks are filled with student-generated notes and Foldables, students have tangible proof of their learning accomplishments.

Independent Foldables: Foldables are often used before, during, and after instruction, instead of or in conjunction with worksheets. They are graded, returned to students, discussed, and frequently used to generate writing activities or to stimulate self-questioning and discussion. They can also be used as an alternative form of assessment and a format for student projects. Keeping these Foldables together in a portfolio or using them to make a project-like study guide assures continued student immersion in the skills taught.

Independent Foldable Projects: For over thirty years Dinah has designed Foldable project formats that students can either write on directly and/or use as a base upon which to collect and display smaller, completed Foldables. Each format becomes a comprehensive collection point for independent Foldables, and the resulting project acts as a thematic, conceptual, and/or chapter-based study guide. The projects formed in this manner are not only beneficial for students as immersive study guides, but they often take the place of portfolios in that they collect and display student work. The same Foldables that are used within Foldable projects can also be glued onto and into the following: bulletin boards, poster boards, charts, display cases, story boards, and any format used for interactive notebooks such as composition books, spiral notebooks, binder paper, and more.

Dependent Foldables: When Foldables are used inside composition books and spiral notebooks as part of student assignments or when they are used within interactive notebooks they become part of the notebook itself. These Foldables usually do not need to be independent at any point in their use in that they are part of a whole -- the notebook -- and they are graded as part of the whole. If this is the case, then these Foldables can be made in a completely different manner, as described on the next page and illustrated throughout this book. This new version of paper-saving Foldables results in manipulatives that are *dependent upon the notebook or project in which they are to be used;* thus, they are called Dependent Foldables or, as Dinah refers to them, Notebook Foldables.

Paper for Independent Foldables: Most Foldables are made using a single sheet of paper folded to form an independent manipulative that has a front section and a back section of paper. When one of these sections is cut, tabs or layers are formed, resulting in an independent kinesthetic graphic organizer like the one pictured to the right.

Front Section

Back Section

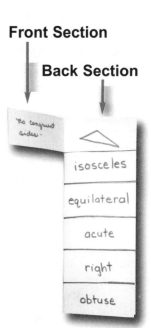

Wasted Paper: When an independent Foldable is glued inside a notebook, both the back side of the back section of paper as well as the paper the Foldable is glued onto are wasted.

Two Ways to Prevent Paper Waste:

1a. Glue can be placed along the back edge of an independent Foldable, close to the fold that allows for the kinesthetic action of the manipulative, and the Foldable can then be glued within a spiral notebook or onto a poster project. When the glue dries, a fold is made along the glue line, and students can write on the back side of the Foldable and on the paper under the Foldable. This technique is illustrated on page 14.

1b. Another version of this same idea has students make a Foldable, and then make an extra fold ½" from the main fold (right), forming a ½" tab. Students then staple along this fold before writing on the Foldable. The ½" tab of this Foldable can be glued into a notebook allowing students to write on the back side of the Foldable and on the paper under the Foldable.

This works well, but it results in a great deal of writing space that is not always needed, and when numerous Foldables are used within a notebook they make the interactive notebook very thick and difficult to use and store.

2. If half of a Foldable is made and glued onto another sheet of paper---for example the paper in a notebook---it results in the same format as an independent Foldable, but it is now dependent upon the paper to which it is glued. Dependent Foldables are really easy to use, and double the available paper in a notebook without making it overly thick and unwieldy.

In this book, Dinah demonstrates how to make dependent Foldables several different ways -- using regular binder paper, using templates to be photocopied, using a CD to generate Foldables in which graphics and copy can be added, and even using sticky notes.

When placing Independent Foldables into spirals or onto poster board projects, the back of the Foldable can be visible and the paper that the Foldable is glued onto can still be used if the Foldable is glued using the following method:

Draw a line of glue along the back fold (mountain fold) of the manipulative.

NOTE: Independent Foldables made using whole sheets of binder paper will not fit within a composition book. If you plan to use this method, students must use spiral notebooks. Also, colored binder paper is used to make the Foldables in this book more visible in the fold instructions and photographs. White, inexpensive paper is typically used to make Foldables.

Position the Foldable onto the right edge of a right page in a spiral notebook. Allow the glue to dry before proceeding.

Fold the entire Foldable to the left along the dried glue line. Students can write on the back of the Foldable and on the notebook paper behind it.

Make a Notebook: Students can make their own notebooks from a stapled stack of notebook paper, photocopy paper, or grid paper.

Collect the number of sheets of paper needed for the notebook.

Staple the sheets together about ½" from the left edge of the stack.   As illustrated in the photo above left, staples can be placed above, below, and between the holes of the binder paper.

To make a decorative spine for the stapled edge, use a 2" x 10½" strip of colored paper for a notebook made of binder paper, or cut a 2" x 11" strip if using stapled photocopy or grid paper. Fold the decorative strip in half along the long axis.

Using a sheet of notebook paper as a guide, punch holes in the decorative strip.

Aligning the holes, glue the strip to the front and back of the left edge of the stapled paper.

This homemade notebook can be stored in a three-ring binder. Multiple notebooks can be made, and the color of the decorative spine can be used to color-code notebooks according to their purpose and use.

Three-hole Binder Paper Notebook Foldables:
Three-hole paper (10½" x 8") can be used to make Foldables that fit within spiral notebooks (10½" x 8"). Because composition books (9¾" x 7½") are smaller, the paper needs to be cut before using it to make Notebook Foldables. The blue paper to the left is a perfect size for making Notebook Foldables. Notice how the vertical margin and horziontal header lines of binder paper can be used as cutting guides.

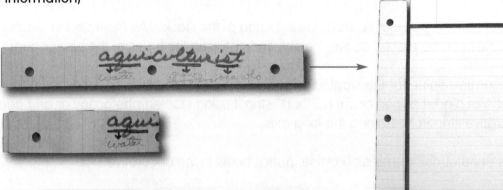

Flat

Folded

Cutting Order Suggestion: First, cut off the vertical margin side with holes to form the long flashcard strips illustrated below. Next, cut off the remaining header section. Both paper strips can be used to make VKVs (Visual Kinesthetic Vocabulary), as illustrated above right and below. (See pages 114 and 115 for more information)

Store on a ring: Line up the end holes as you fold the VKVs in half (above), and store them on a ring (below).

White Binder Paper: Remember that white binder paper (above), photocopy paper, or grid paper is usually used to make Notebook Foldables. Colored binder paper was used in the photographed examples in this book so the Foldables would be visible when glued onto the white paper found in composition books.

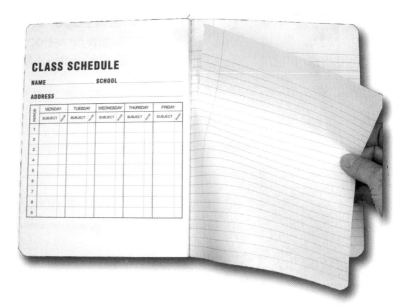

Cutting Example #1

Cutting Example #2

Tear Out Paper to Make Notebook Foldables: Composition books can be purchased at some discount stores for one dollar each. If Foldables are to be used within a composition book, composition book paper can be used to make them. When possible, ask students to purchase one or two extra composition books as part of their school supply list. Collect these books and use the paper from them to make Notebook Foldables.

1. Carefully tear out paper.

2. Trim ½" to 1" from the torn edge. Students might use the red margin line as a trimming guide.

3. Fold the trimmed sheet like a hotdog (along the long axis), and cut along the fold line to make vertical Notebook Foldables.

4. Fold the trimmed sheet like a hamburger (along the short axis), and cut along the fold line to make horizontal Notebook Foldables.

5. Fold an **anchor tab** and use it to glue the vertical or horizontal Foldables into a notebook. Cut the desired number of **information tabs**.

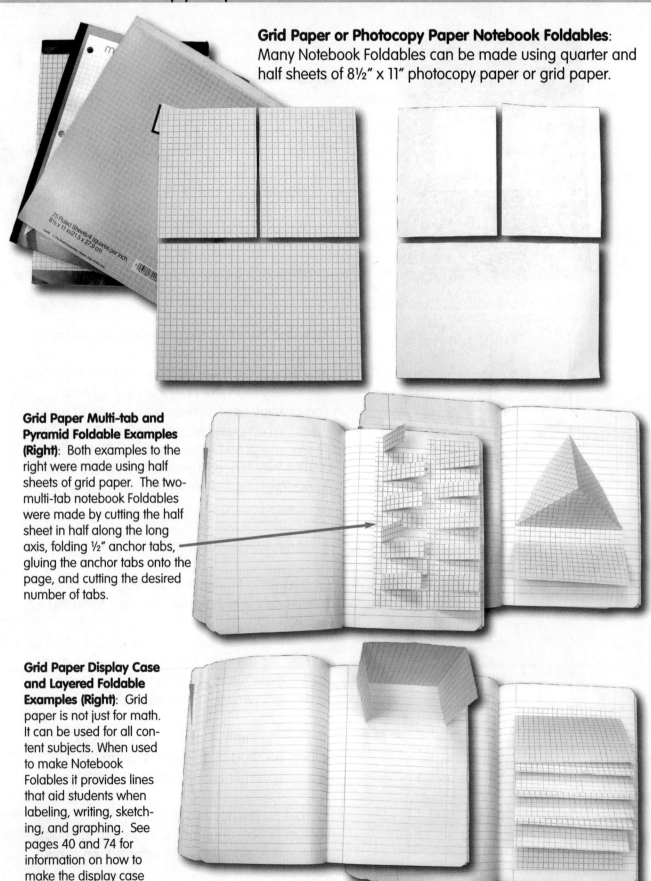

Grid Paper or Photocopy Paper Notebook Foldables:
Many Notebook Foldables can be made using quarter and half sheets of 8½" x 11" photocopy paper or grid paper.

Grid Paper Multi-tab and Pyramid Foldable Examples (Right): Both examples to the right were made using half sheets of grid paper. The two-multi-tab notebook Foldables were made by cutting the half sheet in half along the long axis, folding ½" anchor tabs, gluing the anchor tabs onto the page, and cutting the desired number of tabs.

Grid Paper Display Case and Layered Foldable Examples (Right): Grid paper is not just for math. It can be used for all content subjects. When used to make Notebook Folables it provides lines that aid students when labeling, writing, sketching, and graphing. See pages 40 and 74 for information on how to make the display case and layered Foldables pictured.

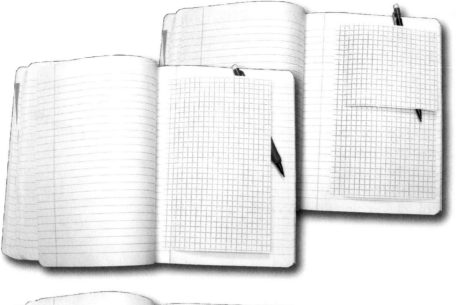

Grid Paper Half-Book and Two-Tab Foldable Examples (Left): Half sheets of grid paper were used to make the one-tab half-book and the two-tab Notebook Foldables pictured.

Photocopy paper is the same size as grid paper and could be used to make all Notebook Foldables pictured on this page and the opposite page.

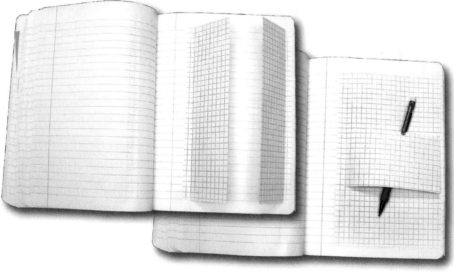

Grid Paper Shutterfold and Three-Tab Foldable Examples (Left): Half sheets of grid paper were used to make both Notebook Foldables pictured. The shutterfold on the left was made by cutting a half sheet of grid paper in half along the long axis to make two equal sections. Anchor tabs were folded along the outer edges and used to glue the front tabs of the shutterfold into the notebook.

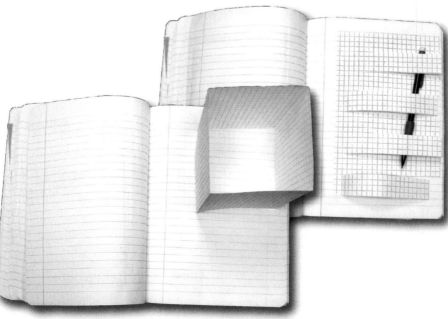

Grid Paper Cube Project and Multi-Tabbed Foldable Examples (Left): Even three-dimensional Foldables like the cube on the left can be made to use within notebooks and can be folded flat when not in use. See page 102 for instructions for making the Cube Notebook Foldable.

Index Card Notebook Foldables: Large (5" x 8"; 127 mm x 203 mm) and small (3" x 5"; 76 mm x 127 mm) index cards can be used to make Notebook Foldables that fit into composition note-books.

Advantages:
- -The cards are a good size and do not have to be trimmed to make most Notebook Foldables.
- -They are sturdy and hold up to frequent use.
- -Writing lines are usually provided on one side.
- -Anchor tabs can be made by folding along the top red margin line.

Disadvantages:
- -Index cards are more expensive than quarter sheets of grid, binder, or photocopy paper.
- -Not readily available
- -The card thickness makes the final notebook very thick.

Index Card Two-Tab and Half-Book Examples (Right): These examples were made using small index cards. This size is more likely to be found at dis-count stores, mak-ing it more cost effective than the larger size.

Index Card Two-Tab and Half-Book Examples (Right): These examples were made using small index cards.

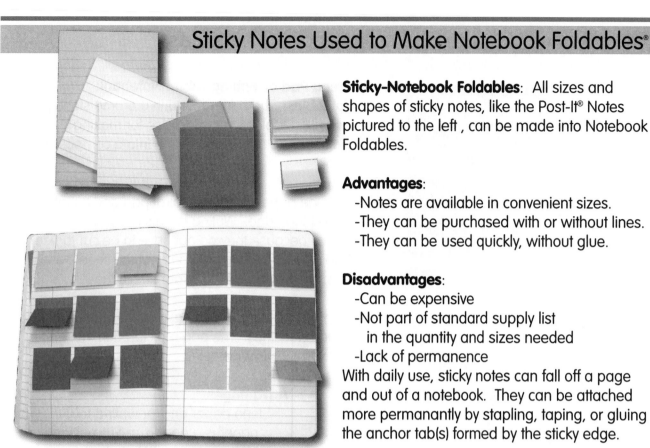

Sticky-Notebook Foldables: All sizes and shapes of sticky notes, like the Post-It® Notes pictured to the left , can be made into Notebook Foldables.

Advantages:
-Notes are available in convenient sizes.
-They can be purchased with or without lines.
-They can be used quickly, without glue.

Disadvantages:
-Can be expensive
-Not part of standard supply list
  in the quantity and sizes needed
-Lack of permanence

With daily use, sticky notes can fall off a page and out of a notebook. They can be attached more permanantly by stapling, taping, or gluing the anchor tab(s) formed by the sticky edge.

Sticky Note Examples (Right): The sticky edge forms the anchor tab. The rest of the sticky note forms the information tab(s).
The student then writes under the tab(s) on the notebook itself.

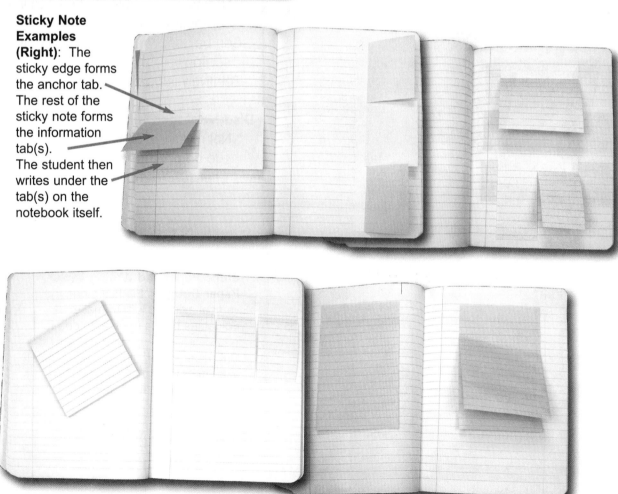

Steno Pad or Writing Tablet Notebook

Foldables: The paper found in a 6" x 9" steno pad or writing tablet is a perfect size for making Notebook Foldables that will fit into a composition book.

Tear the paper out of the spiral pad and cut off the frayed top edge. Writing tablets are advantageous because they do not have to be cut to size. Use whole sheets or fold and cut the sheets as illustrated in the cutting examples to the left.

Steno paper can be purchased with regular or wide-ruled lines. The paper pictured in these examples is wide-ruled.

Advantages:

- Steno paper and/or writing tablet paper is a good size for making Notebook Foldables to be used in a composition book.
- Can be used whole or cut into half sections
- Relatively inexpensive

Disadvantages:

- Not readily available in schools; has to be purchased as a special item

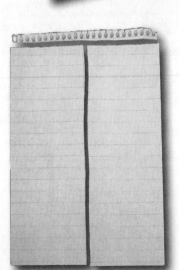

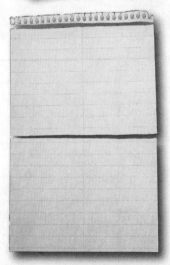

Steno Paper and Writing Tablet

Paper Cuts: Cut in half along the vertical axis (far left) to make Foldables based upon a hotdog fold.

Cut paper in half along the horizontal axis (near left) to make Foldables based upon a hamburger fold.

Vertical Cutting Example   Horizontal Cutting Example

Steno Pad Foldable Examples: The Notebook Foldables pictured in photos a. and b. are made using steno paper cut on the horizontal axis (hamburger) as illustrated in the Vertical Cutting Example on the opposite page.

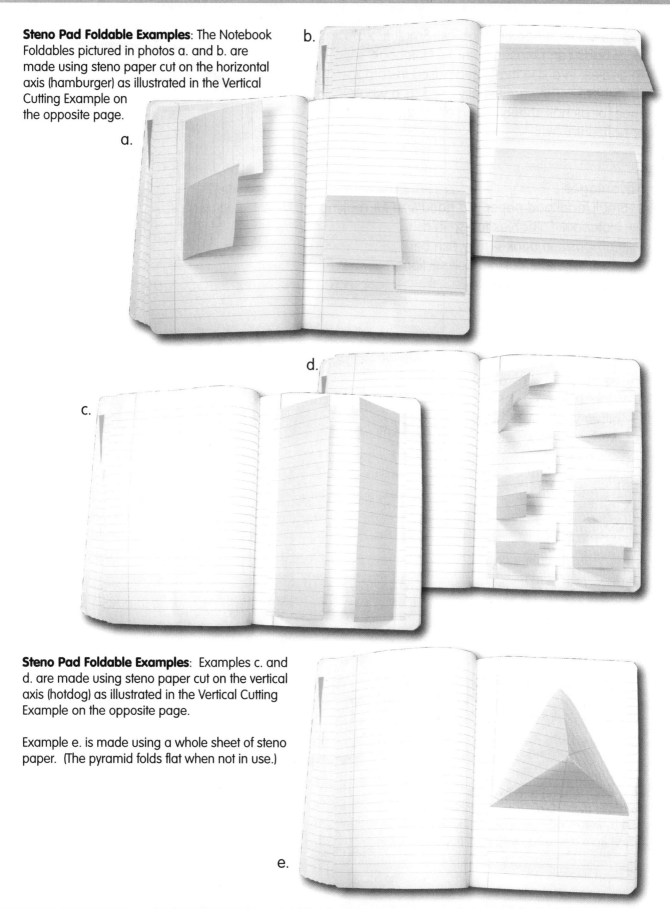

Steno Pad Foldable Examples: Examples c. and d. are made using steno paper cut on the vertical axis (hotdog) as illustrated in the Vertical Cutting Example on the opposite page.

Example e. is made using a whole sheet of steno paper. (The pyramid folds flat when not in use.)

Legal Pad Notebook Foldables: Small 5" x 7" legal pads can be used to make Notebook Foldables, in a size that can be used in composition books. They are usually used as a whole sheet or as half sheets cut on either the vertical or horizontal axis.

Advantages:
- Small legal pad paper is a good size for making Notebook Foldables to use in a composition book -- they can be used whole or cut into half sections.
- Relatively inexpensive.
- No paper is wasted.

Disadvantages:
- Not readily available in schools; has to be purchased as a special item.
- Works best on a vertical axis, while grid paper can be used either vertically or horizontally.

a.

b.

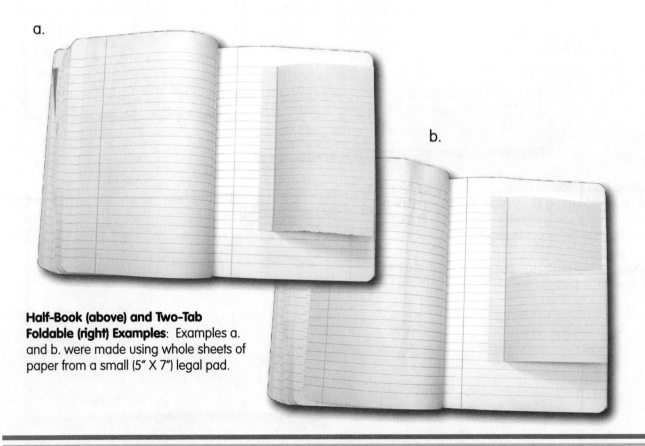

Half-Book (above) and Two-Tab Foldable (right) Examples: Examples a. and b. were made using whole sheets of paper from a small (5" X 7") legal pad.

Pyramid and Three-Tab Foldable Examples:
Examples c. and d. were made using whole sheets of paper from a small legal pad.

c.

d.

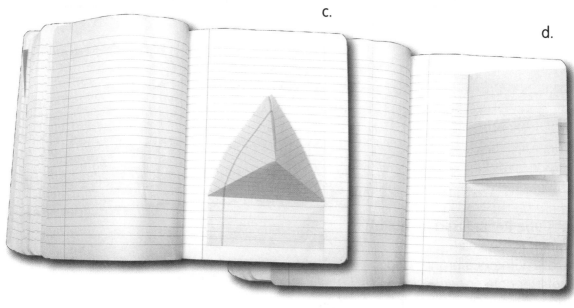

Layered Foldable Example (below):
Example e. was made using half sheets of paper from a small legal pad. The paper was folded in half like a hamburger and cut along the short axis. (See page 40)

f.

e.

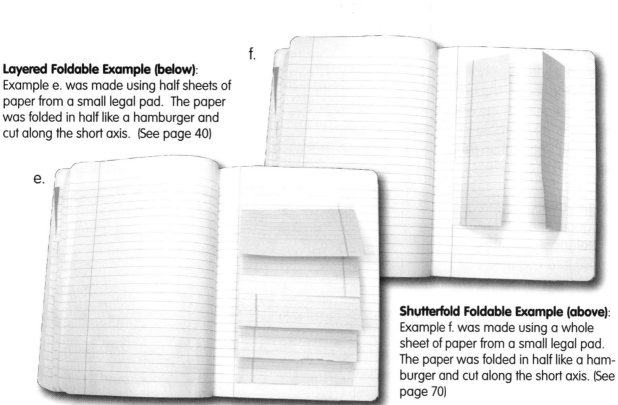

Shutterfold Foldable Example (above):
Example f. was made using a whole sheet of paper from a small legal pad. The paper was folded in half like a hamburger and cut along the short axis. (See page 70)

Paper Cube Refills Used to Make Notebook Foldables:

There are numerous brands and sizes of filler note paper designed for paper cubes. Filler paper (4" x 6", 10.2 cm x 15.2 cm) can be used to made Notebook Foldables.

Use whole sheets or half sheets of cube refill paper. Fold an anchor tab. Place glue on the anchor tab and place the Foldable in the notebook. Cut information tabs if needed. See examples c. and e.

Advantages:
- A good size for making many Notebook Foldables for use in a composition book -- can be used whole or cut into half sections.
- Relatively inexpensive

Disadvantages:
- Not readily available in schools; has to be purchased as a special item
- Not a good size for making shutterfolds, cube projects, and other large Notebook Foldables

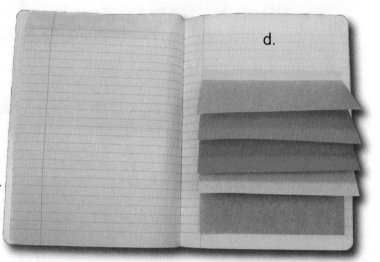

Letter Envelope Pockets: Inexpensive letter envelopes can be purchased at discount stores and used in notebooks. Cut the flap off to make pockets that will hold the following:

- -Index cards
- -Note cards made from quarter sheets of grid or binder paper
- -Worksheets folded into fourths
- -Computer printouts folded into fourths
- -Independent Foldables:
  two-tab, three-tab, Venn diagrams, four-tabs, others
- -Visual Kinesthetic Vocabulary Flashcards (VKVs) (See page 114)

Above: The security envelopes pictured are No. 6, 3¾" x 6½", 9.2 cm x 16.5 cm.

Below: Envelopes of this size can be glued into notebooks on either a horizontal or vertical axis.

Computer Disk Sleeves in Notebooks: Computer disk sleeves, with or without windows, can be used as pockets in notebooks to store any of the following:

- Index cards
- Note cards made from quarter sheets of grid or binder paper
- Worksheets folded into fourths
- Computer printouts folded into fourths
- Independent Foldables: two-tab, three-tab, Venn diagrams, four-tabs, others
- Visual Kinesthetic Vocabulary Flashcards (VKVs) (See page 114)
- Specimen Cards (See page 116)

a. Use to store notecards and flashcards.

b. Use to store folded sheets of paper -- worksheets, computer printouts, information sheets, current events, more.

a.

b.

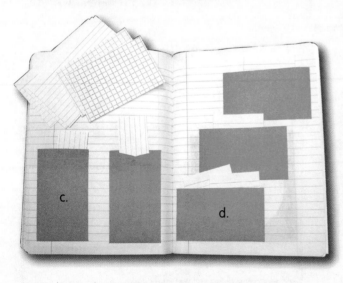

c.

d.

Coin Envelopes in Notebooks: Small 2½" x 4¼" manila envelopes can be used to hold vocabulary cards, math fact cards, small science specimen cards, and more. Seal the envelope and cut off either one of the short edges (example c) or one of the long edges (example d). Use the following to make flashcards:

- Half of a small index card
- An eighth of a sheet of paper
- VKV flashcards made using quartersheets of paper. (See page 114)

Colored-Paper Pocket:

Cut colored paper or scrapbooking paper to make a pocket that fits to the inside of the front or back of the notebook cover. Use 2" clear tape to reinforce the top edge of the pocket before attaching it to the notebook. Place a liberal amount of glue on the other three edges and glue the pocket in place.

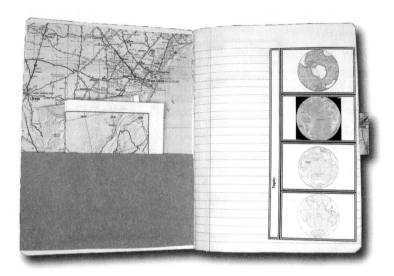

Manila Envelope Pockets in Notebooks:

Cut the flap off a 6" x 9" manila envelope. With the clasp facing you and positioned to the top, shave off the right edge of the envelope. This forms an envelope with an opening along the top and along the right side. Glue the envelope to the inside of the front cover of a notebook. Do the opposite (shave off the left side) for an envelope to be glued to the back cover of a notebook. With the opening of the envelope positioned toward the inner spine of the notebook, objects are less likely to fall out of the pocket and be lost.

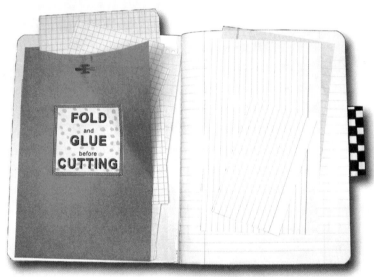

Use this envelope to store 8½" x 11" worksheets or computer printouts that have been folded in half like a hamburger. Use it to store extra sheets or cut sections of notebook paper to be used to make future Foldables.

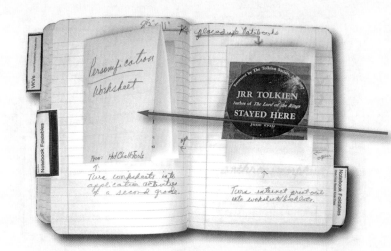

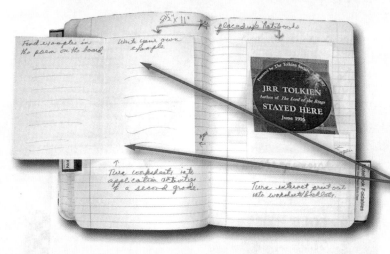

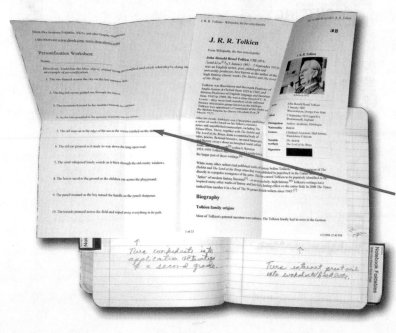

Steps for Turning a Worksheet Into a Notebook Foldable:

Students complete a duplicated worksheet, like the one on personification pictured at left.

Fold the 8.5" x 11" worksheet in half like a hamburger, and fold it again in half like a hamburger, forming a quarter-sheet-sized booklet.

Treat the folded sheet as a booklet. Place the folded spine edge to the left and position the folds of the paper to the top. Students write a title on the front of the newly formed booklet.

The teacher assigns a higher-level thinking activity for students to complete on the inside of their booklet. The activity might extend across both sides, or the two sides can be used for two separate activities. For example, to the inside left, students might be asked to find examples of personification in a poem, and on the other side they might write their own examples of personification.

When closed, the worksheet becomes a student-produced activity, and when opened completely the worksheet is revealed.

Two grades could be taken from this single sheet of paper -- a recognition/recall grade from the inside worksheet, and a production grade from the application and extension seen in student writing on the outside.

Turn A Computer Printout into a Notebook Foldable: Use computer-generated copies of news events, primary source interviews, reference book entries, blogs, and more by folding them into fourths (as described on the previous page) before gluing them into the notebook.

In the example to the right, the top news report on the environment was folded into fourths. It can be glued into a notebook by applying glue to the back as shown.

The second news article could be folded in the same manner and glued on top of the first article to form a two-paper booklet.

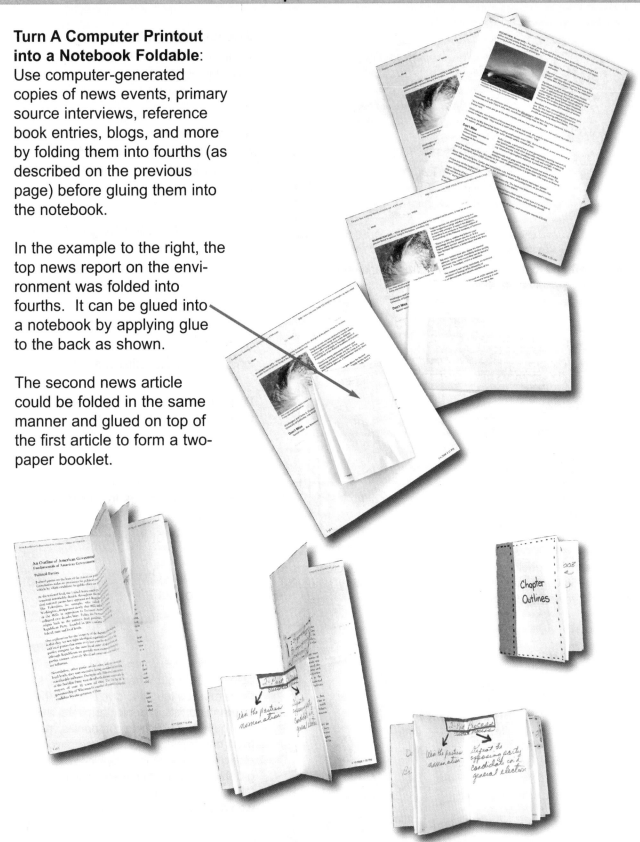

Above: Three information sheets were made into a Foldable booklet by folding them into fourths, gluing the fourths side by side, gluing a spine over the folds, and writing a title on the front. The blank pages formed by the folded sheets can be used to record main ideas and other notes.

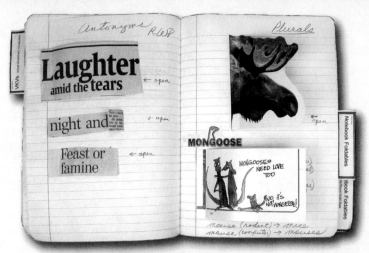

Above Left and Right: Items from magazines and newspapers become tabs within a notebook.

Above Left: The photocopied cover of a piece of literature forms a large tab. Students might be asked to write a summary, synopsis, critique, or review under this tab.

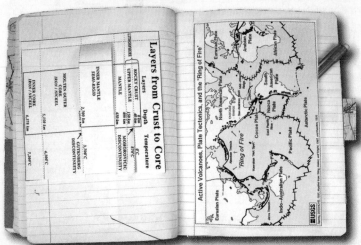

Above Left: A diagram was anchored into the notebook and then cut to form tabs corresponding to the layers of the Earth.

Anchor Tabs on Everything: Graphics, titles, or text from real world print (RWP) can be turned into Notebook Foldables.

Instructions:
Cut out the item to be used in the notebook. Make sure it will fit in the space allocated.

Fold an anchor tab along one edge.

Place glue on the anchor tab and use it to connect the item to a page in the notebook.

Students write in the notebook under and around the affixed item.

Items that can be used as Notebook Foldables include the following:
- Magazine pictures
- Photographs
- Newspaper articles
- Titles or headings from articles
- Diagrams
- Circle, bar, or line graphs
- Maps
- Tables and charts
- Photocopies

Important Note: When using graphics obtained from published print sources, students must be taught to give credit to the following: artists, graphic designers, illustrators, authors, publishing companies, trademark and copyright holders, and anyone else contributing to the graphic. When graphics are used that were generated by fellow students, give credit to the student(s) who developed the graphic aids.

Hints for Using Newspaper and Magazine Articles in Notebooks:

An entire article is often too large to place within a notebook. Have students anchor pictures from the article into their notebooks, or the initial paragraphs that summarize the article. Under the tab formed by the pictures or the paragraphs, students might be asked to write their own summary, synopsis, and/or review. Or they might be asked to make an outline of the article or to record their responses to the information it imparted.

Graphics from Textbooks or Worksheets (Left):

Key graphics found within curriculum aids might be photocopied and anchored into student notebooks. Remember, proper credit must be given to the original source.

Leave a Tab When Cutting (Below):

Note that when the photocopied graphic was cut out, instead of cutting along the line of the graphic, extra paper was left along the top to be used as an anchor tab.

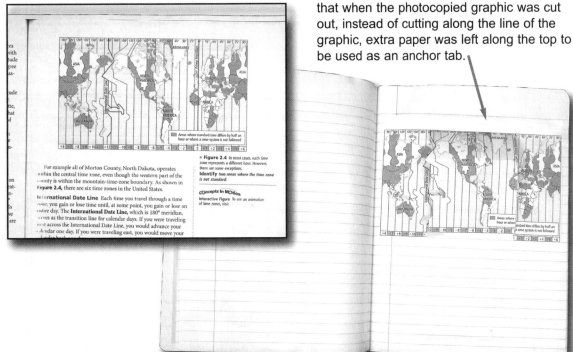

Title:

©2008, DMA; www.dinah.com

Title:

©2008, DMA; www.dinah.com

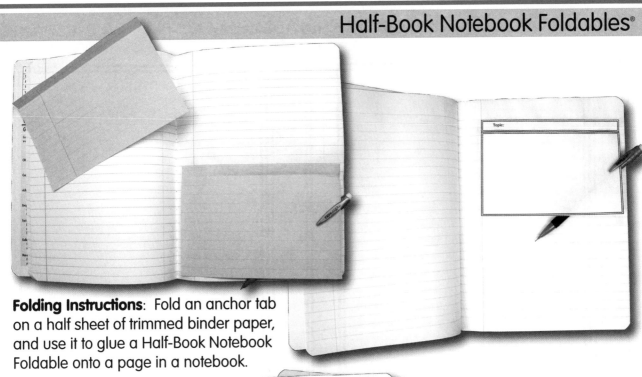

Folding Instructions: Fold an anchor tab on a half sheet of trimmed binder paper, and use it to glue a Half-Book Notebook Foldable onto a page in a notebook.

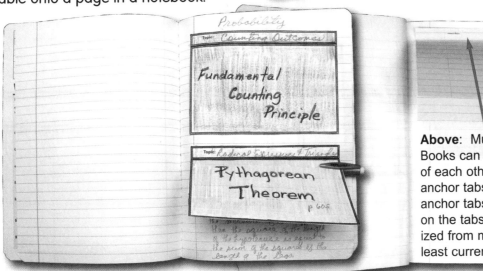

Above: Multiple Half-Books can be glued on top of each other by gluing anchor tabs on top of anchor tabs. Information on the tabs will be organized from most current to least current.

What Goes On, and Under, the Tabs? Main ideas, global concepts, and key questions can be outlined or illustrated on the front tabs. Student responses or study notes can be written underneath.

Make this Notebook Foldable Using Any of the Following:

- half sheets of trimmed binder paper
- quarter sheets of grid or photocopy paper
- small index cards
- large sticky notes
- whole or half sheets of steno paper
- whole or half sheets of small legal pad paper

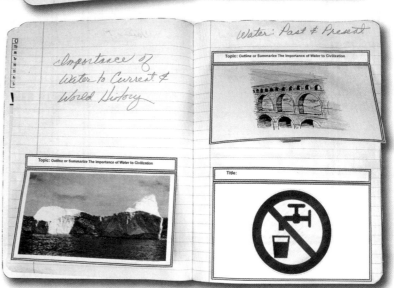

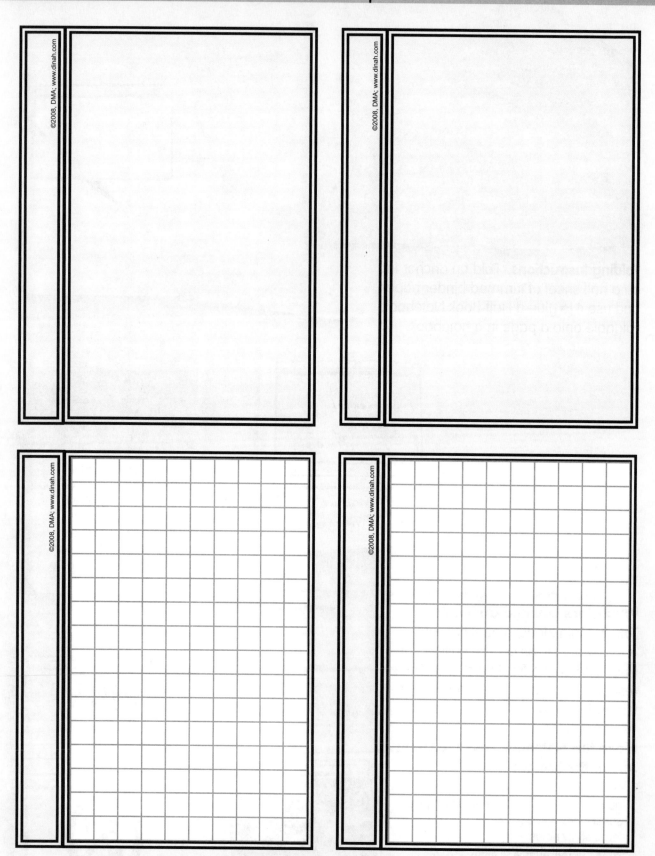

©2008, DMA; www.dinah.com

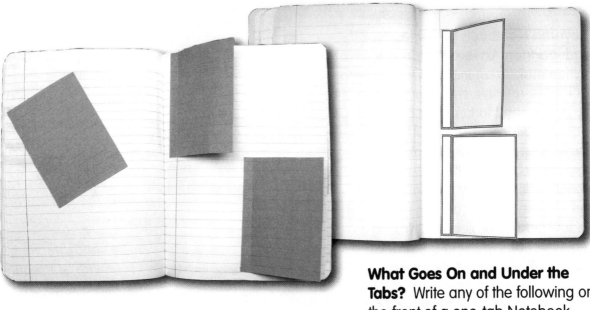

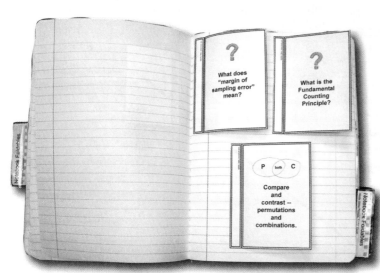

What Goes On and Under the Tabs?

Write any of the following on the front of a one-tab Notebook Foldable:

- -one key vocabulary term
- -one concept or idea
- -one question
- -one quote
- -one theorem or law
- -see lists in *Dinah Zike's Big Books* series for content-specific ideas (See page 9)

Under the tabs have students write any of the following: main and/or supporting ideas, descriptions, definitions, explanations, calculations, questions, opinions, examples, diagrams, quotes, research, summaries, outlines, other responses.

Make this Notebook Foldable Using Any of the Following:

- -quarter sheets of trimmed binder paper
- -eighth sheets of grid or photocopy paper
- -half of a small index card
- -small sticky notes
- -quarter or half sheets of steno paper
- -quarter sheets of small legal pad paper
- -templates featured in this book and CD

Layered Notebook Foldables vs. Independent Layered Foldables: When making an independent layered Foldable, multiple sheets of paper are folded around to form staggered tabs. This is a widely used Foldable. I originally got the idea for this fold from a greeting card fold. It is an effective independent activity that can be used for sequencing, organizing notes, individual student projects, illustrating equivalencies, making bar graphs, giant bulletin boards, and more.

When an independent layered Foldable is glued into a composition book, lots of paper is wasted. Use half-book or one-tab Foldables to make paper-efficient layered Notebook Foldables.

Instructions: All half-book or one-tab Foldables can be glued into a notebook at once as shown in the photograph to the right, or they can be added as different topics are studied or new lessons are begun.

Begin by folding and gluing the anchor tab of the first section of either a half-book or one-tab template or a section of trimmed binder paper. The anchor can be glued along the heading line at the top of the notebook page.

Raise the glued tab and glue the anchor tab of the second tab under the first. Continue this process until the required number of tabs are attached, forming a layered Foldable.

Note: The glued tabs flip forward and backward like an index file.

Above: This layered Notebook Foldable was made using half-sheets of trimmed binder paper. (See page 18) Fold an anchor tab on each section and glue as described in the instructions to the left.

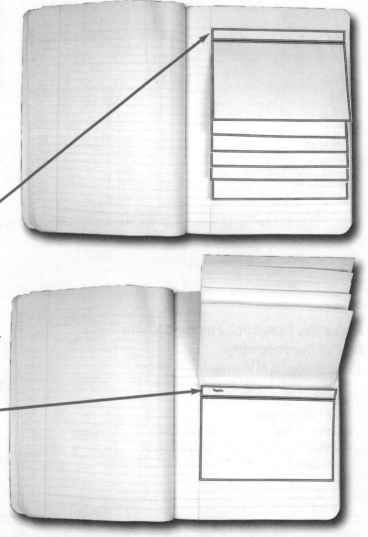

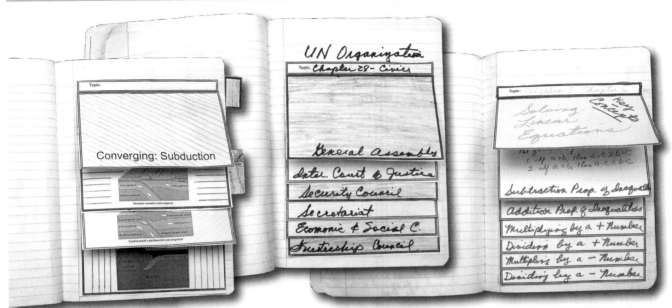

What Goes On and Under the Tabs?

Write any of the following on the front tabs of a layered Notebook Foldable:

- main ideas
- sequential events
- titles of chapter sections or lessons
- countries within a continent
- genres of literature
- names of relevant people, places, things
- see lists in *Dinah Zike's Big Book* series for content-specific ideas (See page 10)

Under the tabs, have students write any of the following: main and/or supporting ideas, descriptions, definitions, explanations, calculations, questions, opinions, examples, diagrams, quotes, research, summaries, outlines, other responses.

Above: Layered Notebook Foldable made using quarter-sheets of trimmed binder paper. (See page 18)

Below: Layered Notebook Foldables made using the one-tab templates featured in this book.

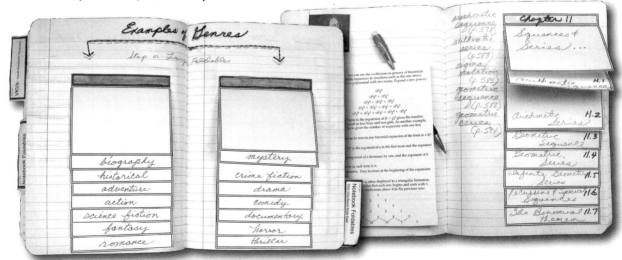

Title:

©2008, DMA; www.dinah.com

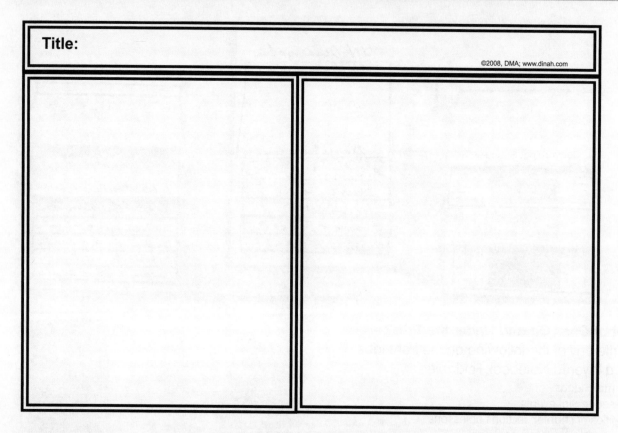

Title:

©2008, DMA; www.dinah.com

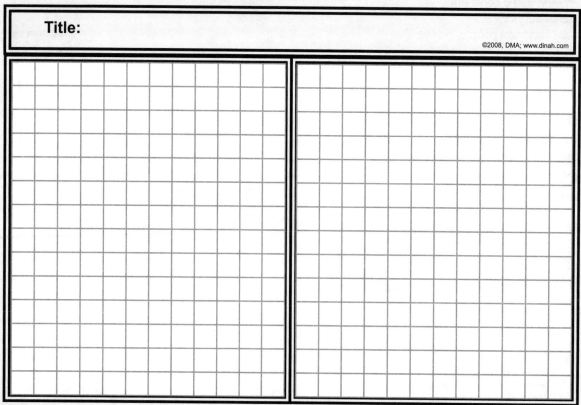

What Goes On and Under the Tabs?

Write any of the following on the front tabs of a two-tab Notebook Foldable:

- two main ideas
- two events
- names of two people, places, things
- two things to be *compared* and *contrasted*
- *cause* and *effect* issues
- *pros* and *cons* of something
- *past* and *present* (or *present* and *future*) views
- see lists in *Dinah Zike's Big Book* series for content-specific ideas to be used with Two-Tab Foldables (See page 10)

Under the tabs, have students write any of the following: main and/or supporting ideas, descriptions, definitions, explanations, calculations, questions, opinions, examples, diagrams, quotes, research, summaries, other responses.

Instructions: Two-tab Notebook Foldables can be made using the templates (left) or horizontal or vertical half sheets of trimmed binder or grid paper (above). (See page 18)

Fold an anchor tab, fold the paper in half to form two information tabs, glue the anchor tab onto a page in the notebook, and cut along the fold line to form two information tabs.

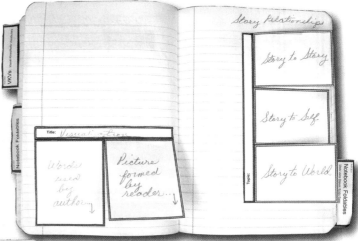

Title:

Title:

Instructions: Three-tab Notebook Foldables can be made using the templates to the left or vertical half-sheets of trimmed binder or grid paper. (See page 18)

Fold an anchor tab. Fold the paper into thirds. Glue the anchor tab onto a page in a notebook. When the glue is dry, cut along the fold lines to form three information tabs.

What Goes On, and Under, the Tabs?

Write any of the following on the front tabs of a three-tab Notebook Foldable:

-three main ideas, topics, categories, or parts
-three important terms
-names of three people, places, things
-**K**now, **W**ant to know, **L**earned
-past, present, future
-beginning, middle, ending (first, next, last)
-see lists in *Dinah Zike's Big Book* series for content-specific ideas (See page 10)

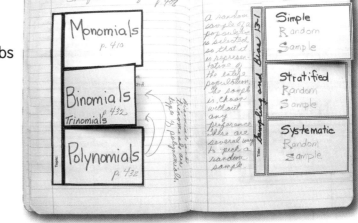

Under the tabs, have students write any of the following:
main and/or supporting ideas, descriptions, definitions, explanations, calculations, questions, opinions, examples, diagrams, quotes, research, summaries, outlines, other responses.

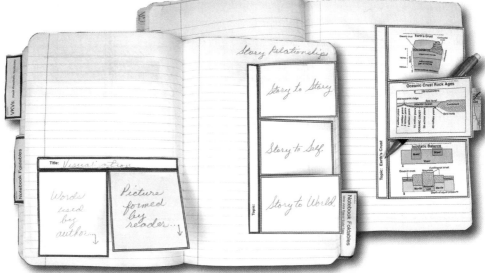

Title:

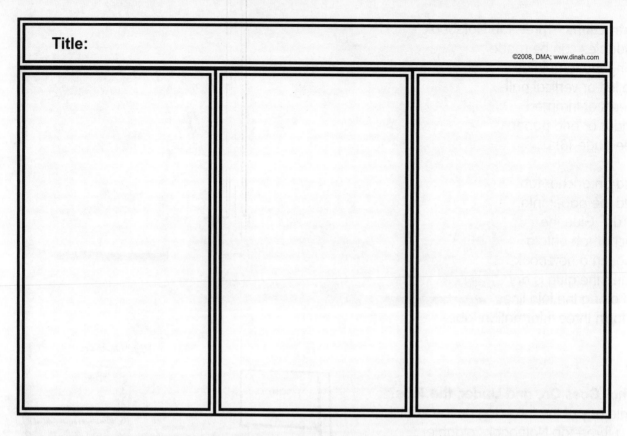

Title:

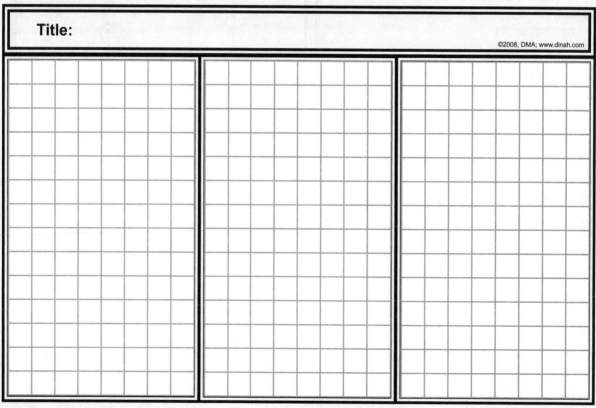

Instructions: Three-tab Notebook Foldables can be made using the templates to the left or horizontal half sheets of trimmed binder or grid paper. (See page 18)

Fold an anchor tab. Fold the paper into thirds. Glue the anchor tab onto a page in a notebook before cutting along the fold lines to form three information tabs.

What Goes On and Under the Tabs?

Write any of the following on the front tabs of a three-tab Notebook Foldable:
  -three main ideas or categories -- igneous, metamorphic, sedimentary rock
  -three skills being studied -- fractions, decimals, percentages
  -three key terms -- sine, cosine, tangent
  -three laws or theorems -- Isaac Newton's Three Laws of Motion
  -three parts of speech -- prefixes, suffixes, root words
  -names of three people, places, things -- three leaders of the Civil Rights Movement
  -**K**now, **W**ant to know, **L**earned
  -past, present, future view on genetic engineering
  -beginning, middle, ending (first, next, last)
  -see lists in *Dinah Zike's Big Book* series for
    content-specific ideas (See page 10)

Under the tabs, have students write any of the following: main and/or supporting ideas, descriptions, definitions, explanations, calculations, questions, opinions, examples, diagrams, quotes, research, summaries, outlines, other responses.

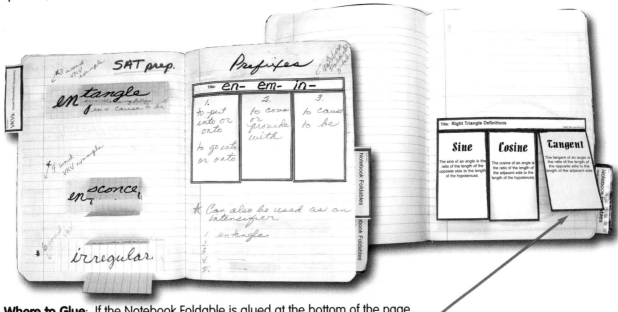

Where to Glue: If the Notebook Foldable is glued at the bottom of the page, students can write on the back of each of the three tabs when they are opened.

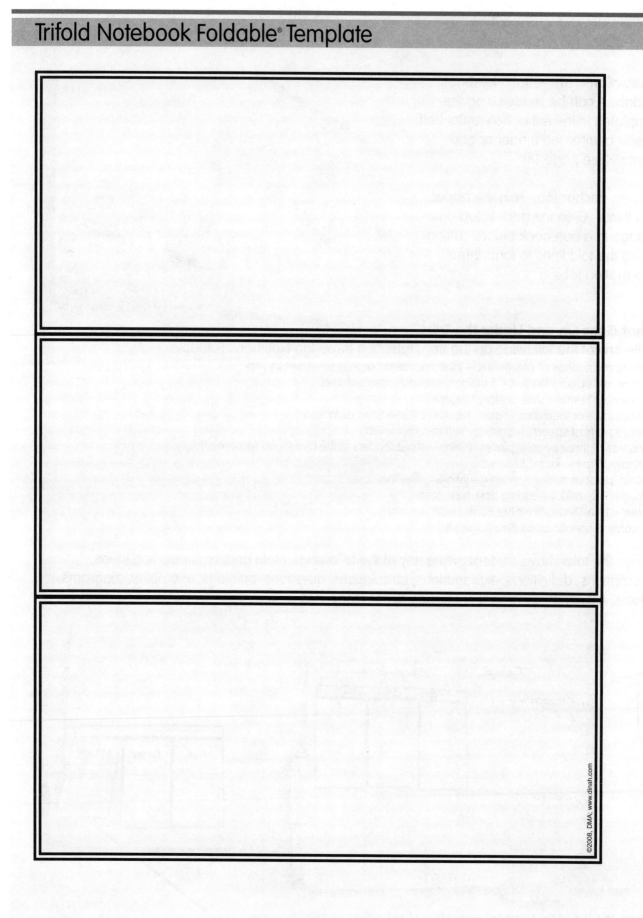

Instructions: Use a full sheet of trimmed binder paper or grid paper, or use a sheet of either steno paper, writing tablet paper, or small legal pad paper. Fold the selected paper into thirds as illustrated. To avoid dried glue bulges when writing in the middle of the Notebook Foldable, glue the center section of the Trifold into the notebook by placing glue on the outer left and right edges of the central section. Fold the trifold tabs so that they overlap in the middle to make room to write on the notebook page above and below the Foldable.

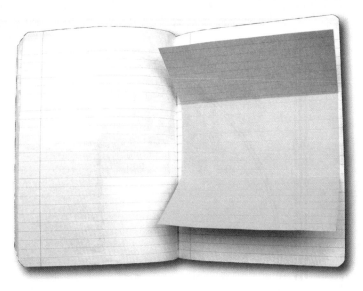

What Goes On and Under the Tabs?

Write both titles/objectives and information on the front tabs of trifold Notebook Foldables. Titles might include:

- three main ideas or categories -- executive, legislative, judicial branches of government
- three skills -- AAS (angle, angle, side), SAS (side, angle, side), SSS (side, side, side)
- three key terms or concepts -- water cycle, nitrogen cycle, oxygen cycle
- names of three people, places, things -- three main or supporting characters in a novel or story
- **K**now, **W**ant to know, **L**earned
- past, present, future -- views of women in the American work force
- beginning, middle, ending (first, next, last) of a short story or an event in history
- before, during, after -- information on events, opinions, or ideals over time
- see lists in *Dinah Zike's Big Book* series for content-specific ideas (See page 10)

On the labeled tabs have students write any of the following: main and/or supporting ideas, descriptions, definitions, explanations, calculations, questions, opinions, examples, diagrams, quotes, research, summaries, outlines, other responses.

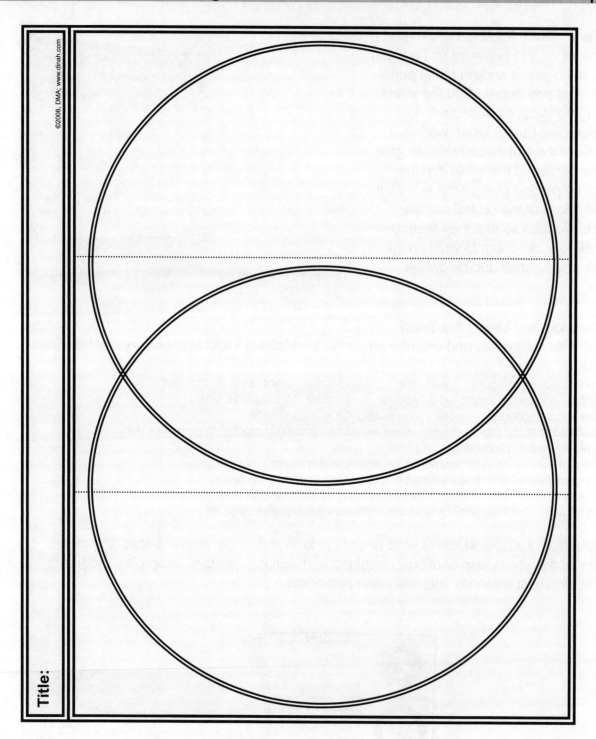

©2008, DMA; www.dinah.com

Title:

Instructions: Use a full sheet of trimmed binder paper or grid paper, or use a sheet of steno paper, writing tablet paper, or small legal pad paper.

Fold an anchor tab. Fold the selected paper into thirds. Draw a Venn Diagram that overlaps in the middle of the three-folds. Glue the anchor tab onto a page in a notebook. When the glue is dry, cut along the fold lines to form three information tabs (right).

(See section entitled **What Goes On and Under the Venn Diagram Tabs?** on page 51)

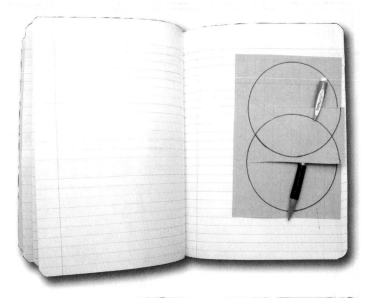

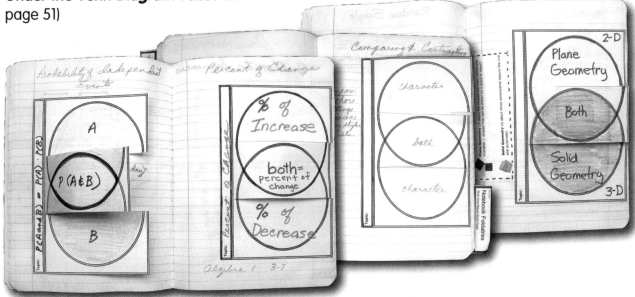

Title:

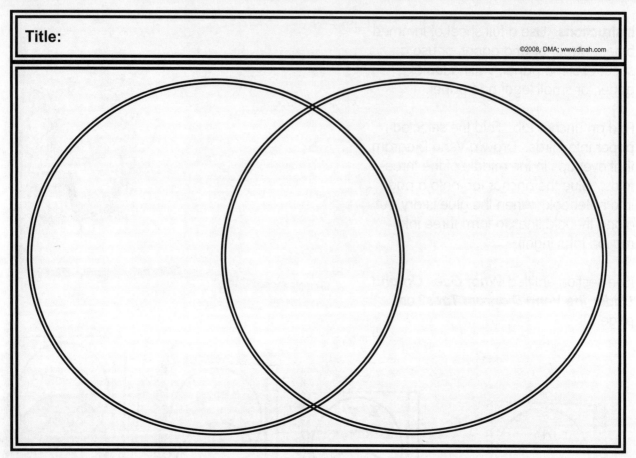

Title:

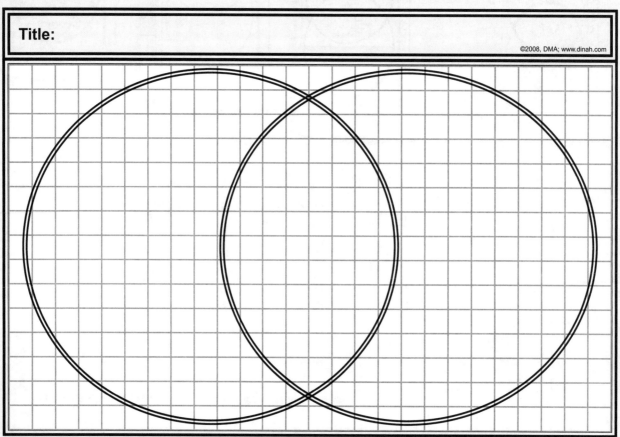

What Goes On and Under the Venn Diagram Tabs?

On the front outer tabs, label the two things that are to be compared and contrasted, and label the middle tab "Both." Use the Venn diagram to compare any of the following:

- two people, locations, events, opinions
- fractions, decimals, both
- two novels by the same author
- Federalists, Anti-Federalists, both
- two periods of Anti-Federalism
- % of increase, % of decrease, both (the % of change)
- character #1, character #2, both
- plane geometry, solid geometry, both
- Puritans, Quakers, both
- Teddy Roosevelt, F.D. Roosevelt, both
- see lists in *Dinah Zike's Big Book* series for content-specific ideas (See page 10)

Under the tabs have students write the characteristics or traits of the items listed on the front of the two outer tabs, and list or describe what they have in common under the middle tab.

(See section entitled ***Instructions*** on page 49)

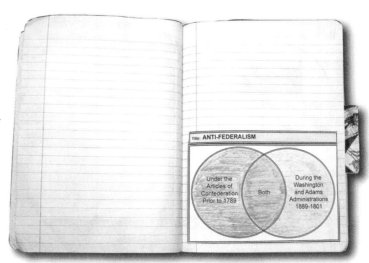

Make Vertical and/or Horizontal Venn Diagram Notebook Foldables Using any of the Following:

- half sheets of trimmed binder paper
- half sheets of grid or photocopy paper
- small index cards
- three small sticky notes
- half sheets of steno paper or writing tablet paper
- whole sheet of small legal pad paper

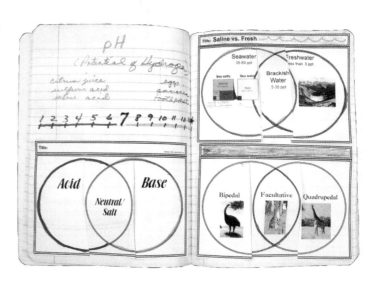

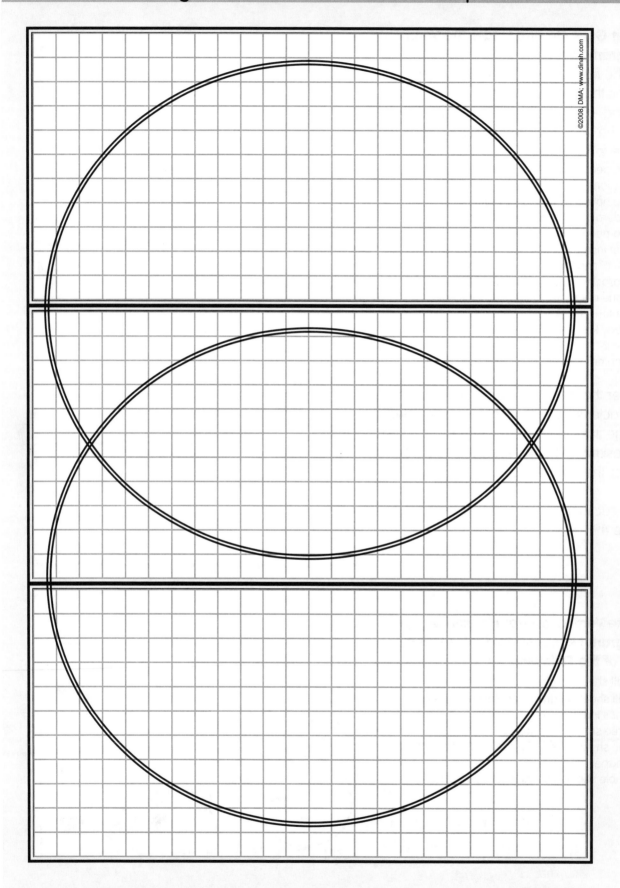

©2008 DMA; www.dinah.com

Instructions: Use either the template to the left, a sheet of trimmed binder paper, a sheet of trimmed grid paper, or a sheet of either steno paper, writing tablet paper, or small legal pad paper to make the trifold pictured left. Fold the selected paper into thirds as illustrated to the right. To avoid glue spots that are difficult to write over in the middle section, place thin lines of glue along the outer left and right edges of the middle section. Glue the Foldable onto the middle of a notebook page. Fold the Trifold inward to make room to write on the notebook page above and below the Foldable.

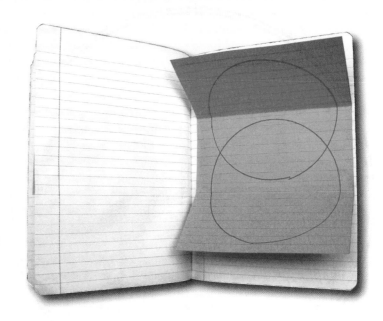

What Goes On and Under the Tabs?

On the outer tabs, label two things to be compared and contrasted, and label the middle tab "Both." Write about commonalities in the middle section of the Venn diagram Trifold:

- House of Representatives, Senate, both form the Congress (This is a *merger*. See Dinah Zike's website for more information on mergers, www.dinah.com.)
- two dimensional figures, three-dimensional figures, both
- see lists in *Dinah Zike's Big Book* series for content-specific ideas (See page 10)

On the tabs front of the three sections, have students write the characteristics or traits of the items listed on the two outer tabs, and list or describe what they have in common on the front of the middle tab.

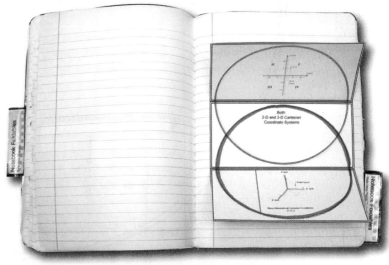

What Goes On and Under the Tabs?

Arrange the diagram circles to illustrate any of the following: Venn diagrams, sets of information to be compared and contrasted, or parts or layers of circular objects (Earth's layers, atmospheric layers, layers of the Sun or planets in the Solar System).

The examples below are listed from the largest to the smallest sets.

- rational numbers, integers, whole numbers, natural numbers
- plot, subplot(s)
- see lists in *Dinah Zike's Big Book* series for content-specific ideas (See page 10)

Under the tabs, have students respond to and/or explain the data represented by the parts of the diagram.

Above: Circle templates can be used directly in student notebooks or as patterns for cutting circles from colored paper.

Below: Fold circles in half and glue only half of the tab down to form half-circle tabs.

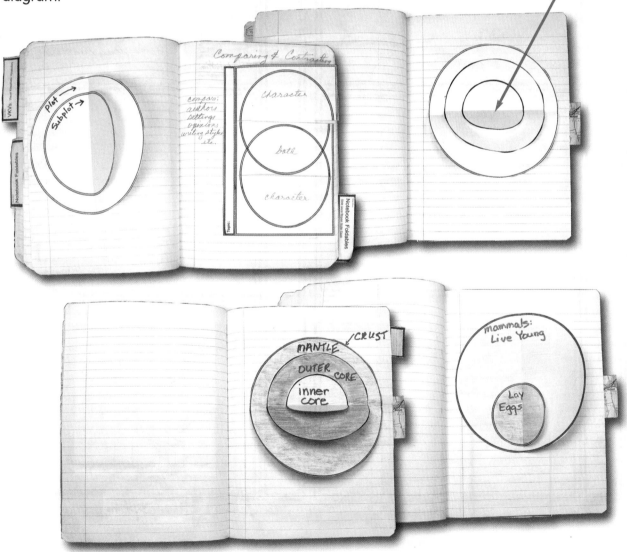

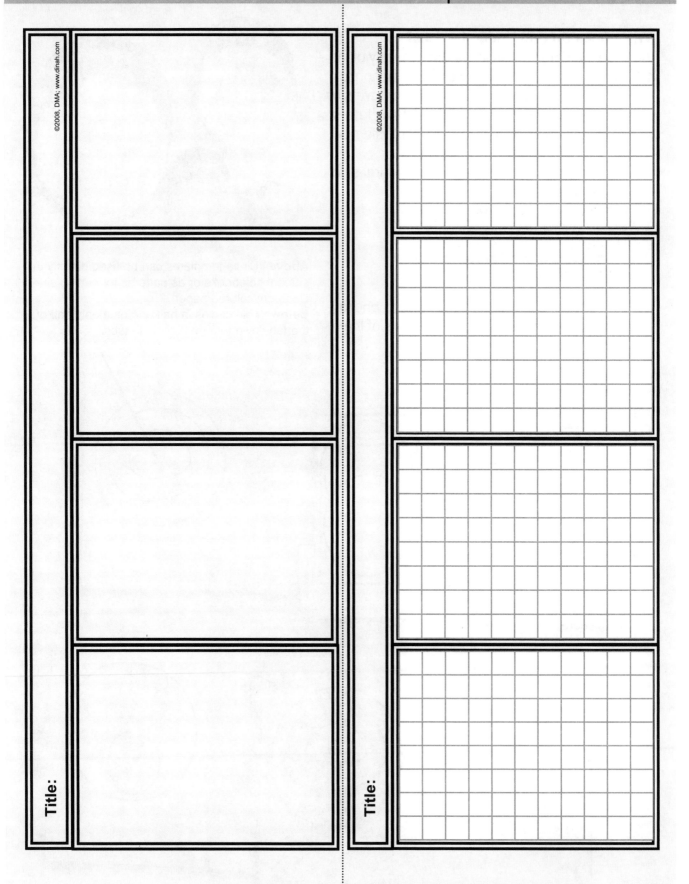

©2008, DMA; www.dinah.com

Title:

©2008, DMA; www.dinah.com

Title:

Instructions: Four-tab Notebook Foldables can be made using the templates to the left or vertical half sheets of trimmed binder or grid paper. See page 18. Fold an anchor tab. Fold the paper into fourths. Glue the anchor tab onto a page in a notebook. Cut along the fold lines to form four information tabs.

What Goes On and Under the Tabs?

Write any of the following on the front tabs of four-tab Notebook Foldables:
- four main ideas or categories
  Organic Molecules: carbohydrates, lipids, proteins, nucleic acids
- four skills or concepts studied
- four key terms
- four steps -- writing equations
- names of four people, places, things --
- **K**now, **W**ant to know, **L**earned, **H**ow it will be used
- see lists in *Dinah Zike's Big Book* series for content-specific ideas (See page 10)

Under the tabs, have students write any of the following: main and/or supporting ideas, descriptions, definitions, explanations, calculations, questions, opinions, examples, diagrams, quotes, research information, summaries, outlines, other responses.

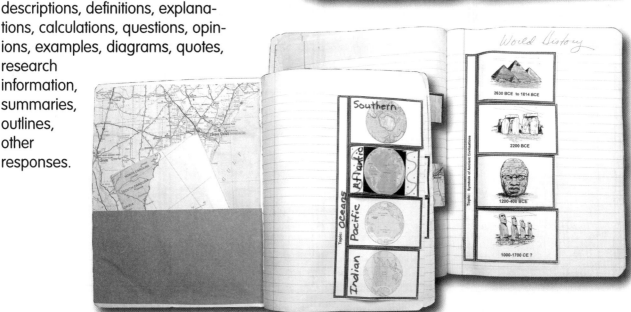

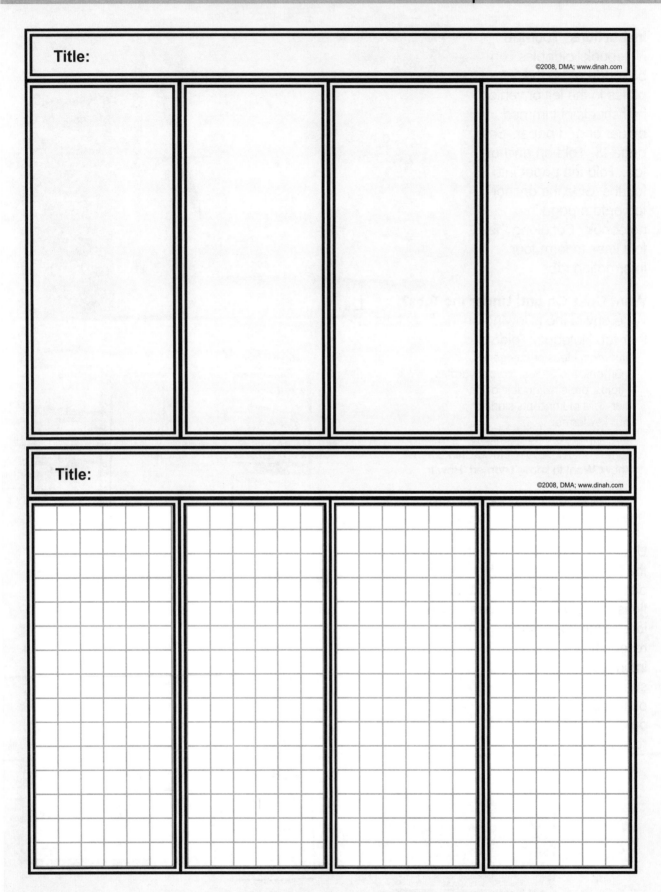

Title:

©2008, DMA; www.dinah.com

Title:

©2008, DMA; www.dinah.com

Instructions: Four-tab Notebook Foldables can be made using the templates to the left or horizontal half sheets of trimmed binder or grid paper. (See page 18)

Fold an anchor tab. Fold the paper into fourths. Glue the anchor tab onto a page in a notebook. Cut along the fold lines to form four information tabs.

What Goes On and Under the Tabs?

Write any of the following on the front tabs of a four-tab Notebook Foldable:
- four dates
- four events
- four main ideas or categories
- four skills or concepts studied
- four key terms
- four steps or parts
- four turning points
- names of four people, places, things
- four questions: **W**ho? **W**hat? **W**hen? **W**here?
- **K**now, **W**ant to know, **L**earned, **H**ow it will be used
- see lists in *Dinah Zike's Big Book* series for content-specific ideas (See page 10)

Under the tabs, have students write any of the following: main and/or supporting ideas, descriptions, definitions, explanations, calculations, questions, opinions, examples, diagrams, quotes, research information, summaries, outlines, other responses.

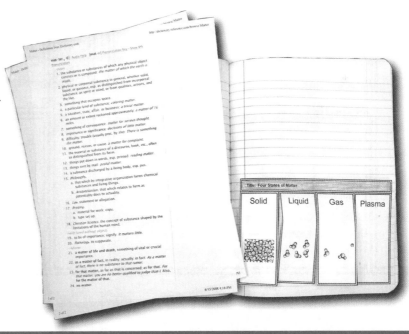

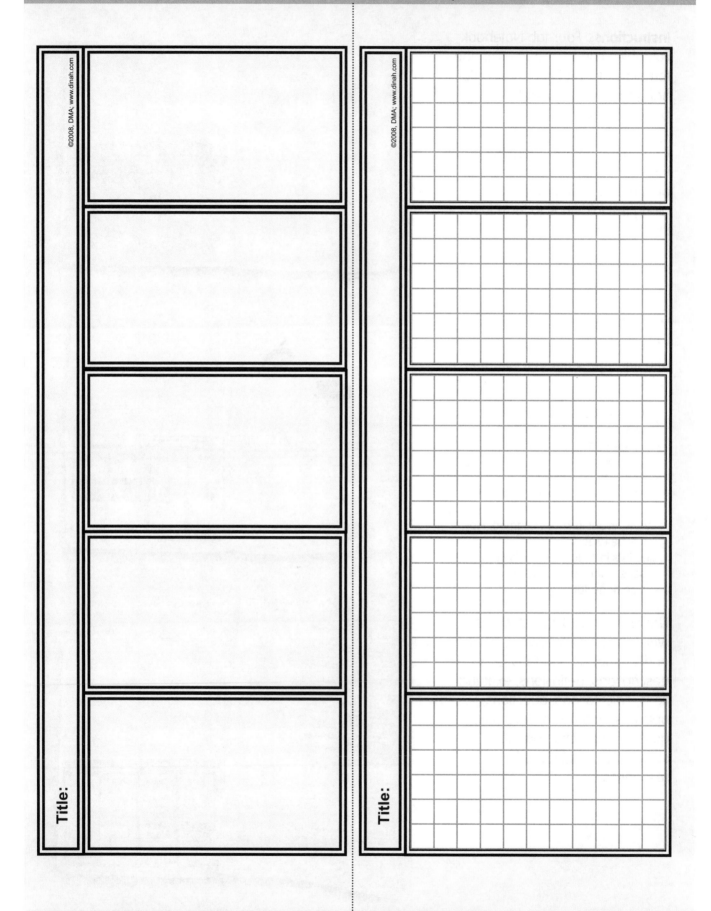

Title:

Title:

©2008, DMA; www.dinah.com

©2008, DMA; www.dinah.com

Instructions: Five-tab Notebook Foldables can be made using the templates to the left or vertical half sheets of trimmed binder or grid paper. (See page 18)

Fold an anchor tab. Fold the paper into fifths. Glue the anchor tab onto a page in a notebook. Cut along the fold lines to form five information tabs.

What Goes On and Under the Tabs?

Write any of the following on the front tabs of a five-tab Notebook Foldable:
- five questions -- **W**ho? **W**hat? **W**hen? **W**here? **W**hy? or **H**ow?
- five important events, people, or things
- five steps or stages
- five key terms
- five parts or pieces -- Atlantic, Pacific, Indian, Arctic, Antarctic (Southern)
- see lists in *Dinah Zike's Big Book* series for content-specific ideas (See page 10)

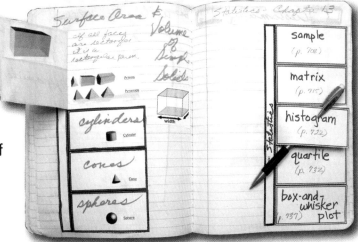

Under the tabs, have students write any of the following: main and/or supporting ideas, descriptions, definitions, explanations, calculations, questions, opinions, examples, diagrams, quotes, research information, summaries, outlines, other responses.

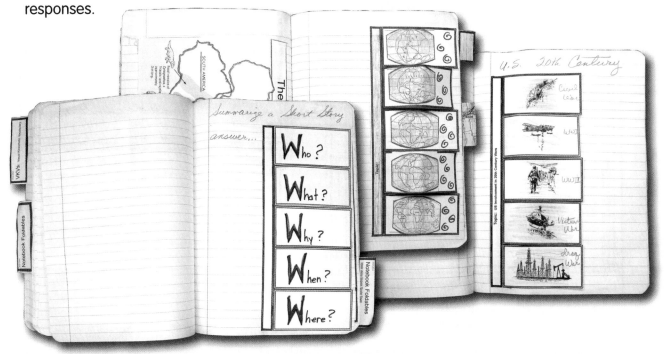

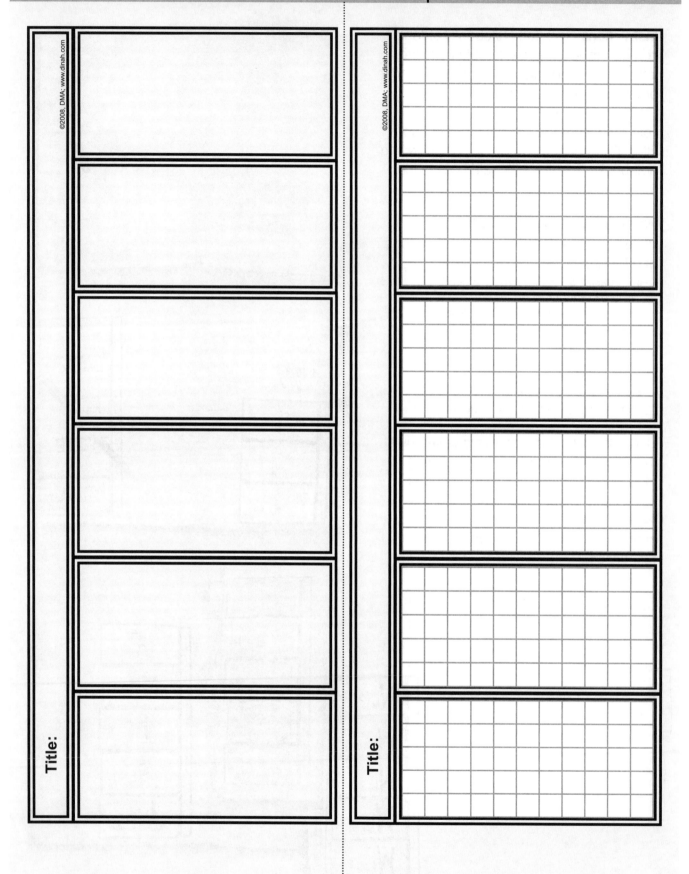

©2008, DMA; www.dinah.com

©2008, DMA; www.dinah.com

Title:

Title:

What Goes On and Under the Tabs?

Write any of the following on the front tabs of a six-tab Notebook Foldable:

- six main ideas or categories
- six skills or concepts being studied
- six key terms
- six steps -- writing equations
- names of six people, places, and/or things
- see lists in *Dinah Zike's Big Book* series for content-specific ideas (See page 10)

Under the tabs, have students write any of the following: main and/or supporting ideas, descriptions, definitions, explanations, calculations, questions, opinions, examples, diagrams, quotes, research information, summaries, outlines, other responses.

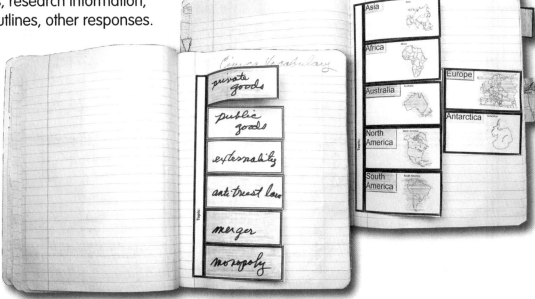

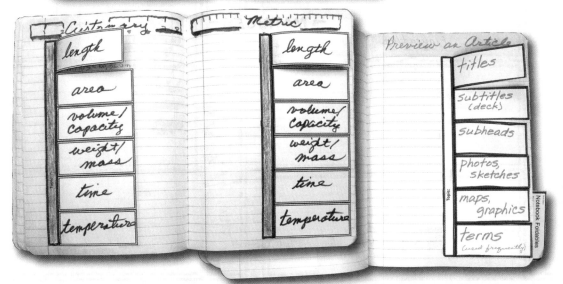

©2008, DMA; www.dinah.com

©2008, DMA; www.dinah.com

Title:

Title:

Instructions: Eight-tab Notebook Foldables can be made using the templates to the left or vertical half sheets of trimmed binder or grid paper. (See page 18)

Fold an anchor tab. Fold the paper into fourths; fold it in half again to form eighths. Glue the anchor tab onto a page in a notebook. Cut along the fold lines to form eight information tabs.

Fewer Folds: Fold an anchor tab. Fold the paper into fourths. Glue the anchor tab onto a notebook page. Cut along the fold lines to form four tabs. Cut each of the tabs in half to form eight tabs.

What Goes On and Under the Tabs? Write any of the following on the front tabs of an eight-tab Notebook Foldable:

- -eight main ideas or categories
- -eight skills being studied
- -eight key terms
- -eight dates
- -eight sequential events
- -names of eight people, places, and/or things
- -see lists in *Dinah Zike's Big Book* series for content-specific ideas (See page 10)

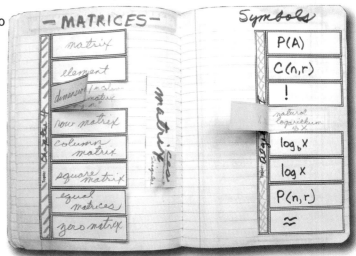

Under the tabs have students write any of the following: main and/or supporting ideas, descriptions, definitions, explanations, calculations, questions, opinions, examples, diagrams, quotes, research information, summaries, other responses.

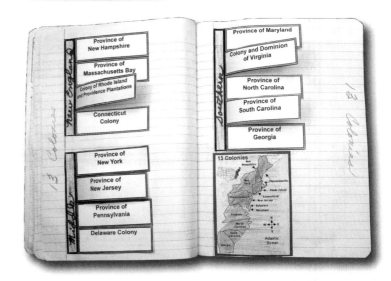

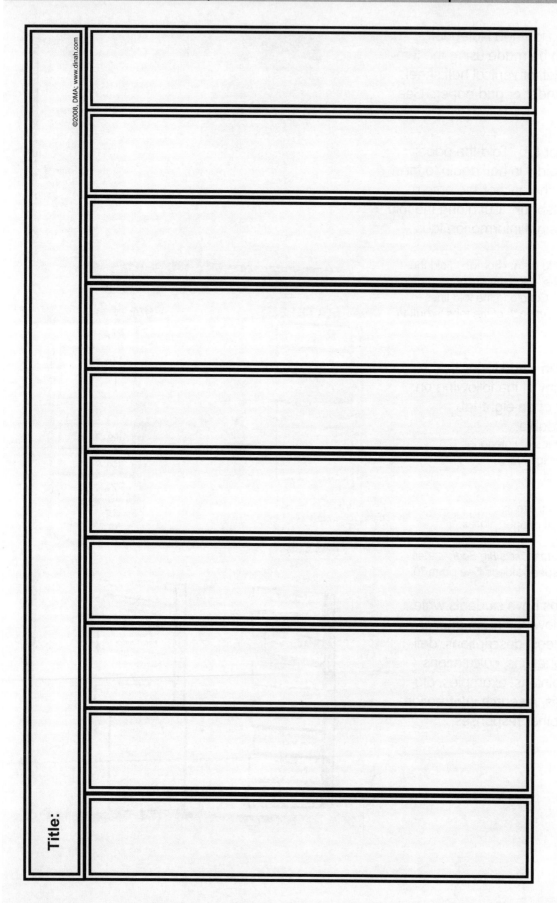

©2008, DMA, www.dinah.com

Title:

Instructions: Ten-tab Notebook Foldables can be made using the templates to the left or vertical half sheets of trimmed binder or grid paper. (See page 18)

Fold an anchor tab. Fold the paper into fifths. Fold the fifths in half to form tenths. Glue the anchor tab onto a page in a notebook before cutting along the fold lines to form ten information tabs.

What Goes On and the Under the Tabs? Write any of the following on the front tabs of a ten-tab Notebook Foldable:
- ten main ideas, categories, skills
- ten key terms or important people
- ten dates and/or sequential events
- ten acronyms, initializations, Greek root words

Under the tabs, have students write brief descriptions, short definitions, sentences using terms, dictionary pronunciations, and more.

©2008, DMA; www.dinah.com

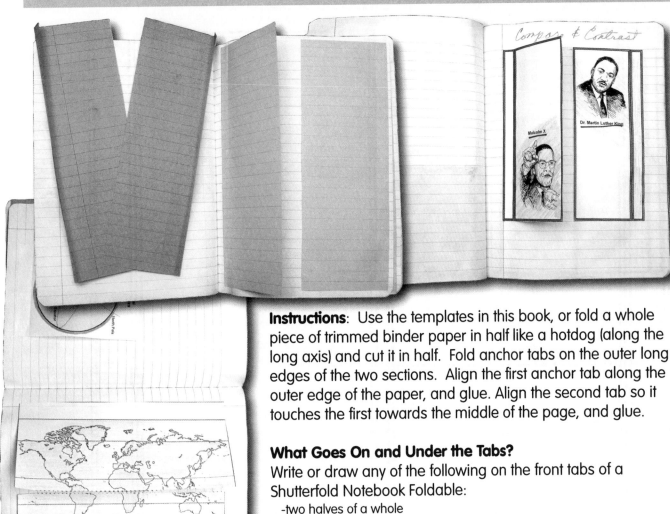

Instructions: Use the templates in this book, or fold a whole piece of trimmed binder paper in half like a hotdog (along the long axis) and cut it in half. Fold anchor tabs on the outer long edges of the two sections. Align the first anchor tab along the outer edge of the paper, and glue. Align the second tab so it touches the first towards the middle of the page, and glue.

What Goes On and Under the Tabs?

Write or draw any of the following on the front tabs of a Shutterfold Notebook Foldable:

- -two halves of a whole
- -two things to compare and contrast; opposites
- -two associated terms -- permutations, combinations
- -two halves of a diagram or map -- equator divides hemispheres

Under the tabs, have students take notes, draw diagrams, record information and terms, or other responses.

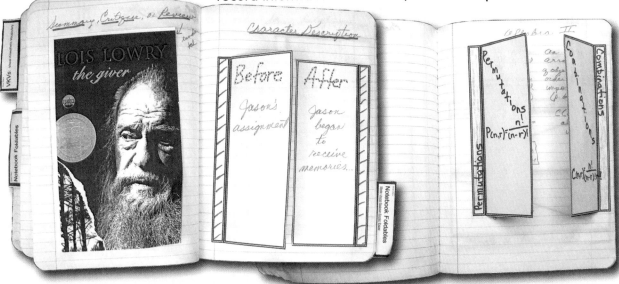

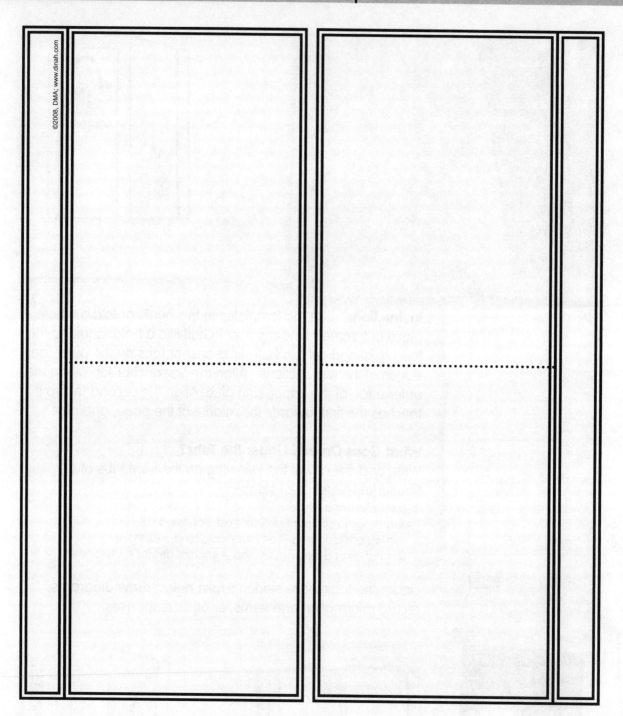

©2008, DMA; www.dinah.com

Instructions: Use the templates in this book, or fold a whole piece of trimmed binder paper in half like a hotdog (along the long axis) and cut it in half. Fold these sections in half as illustrated (right). Fold anchor tabs on the outer long edges of the two sections. Align the first anchor tab along the outer edge of the paper, and glue. Align the second tab so it touches the first towards the middle of the page, and glue. Cut the sections in half along the fold lines.

What Goes On, and Under, the Tabs? Write any of the following on the front tabs of the four-door Notebook Foldable:

- four main ideas, categories, skills -- four Monotheistic religions
- four key terms
- parts of a four-step cycle, or four cycles
- **K**now, **W**ant to know, **L**earned, **H**ow it will be used
- four questions: **W**ho? **W**hat? **W**hen? **W**here?

Under the tabs, have students take notes, draw diagrams, record information and terms, or other responses.

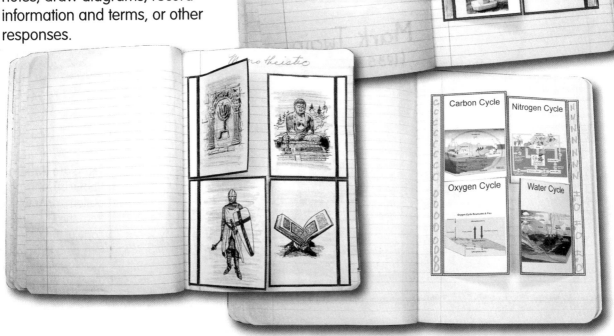

©2008, DMA; www.dinah.com

Glue this side of this tab to the center of the heading
section of a page in a notebook.
Center the tab before gluing.

Template Pattern:
Photocopy this display
pattern, print this pattern
from the CD, or use a
copy of the printed pat-
tern as a template to cut
multiple displays out of
white or colored paper.

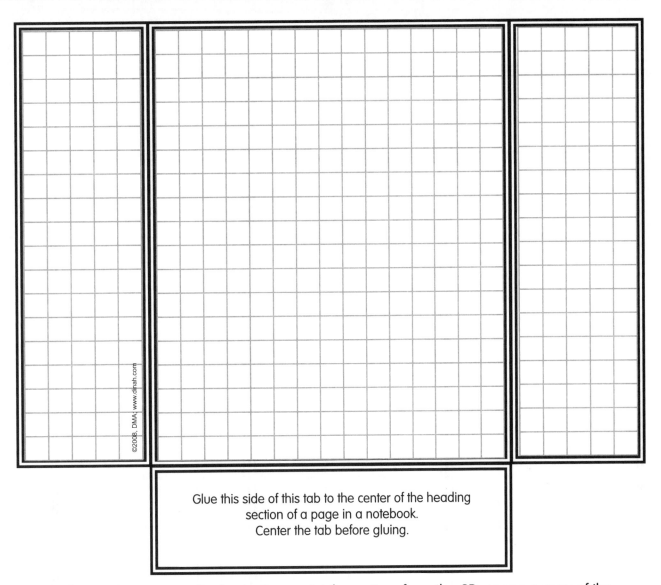

Glue this side of this tab to the center of the heading
section of a page in a notebook.
Center the tab before gluing.

©2008, DMA; www.dinah.com

Instructions: Photocopy a display pattern, print the pattern from the CD, or use a copy of the printed pattern as a template to cut multiple displays out of colored paper. (See example at the bottom of the previous page.) After drawing or writing on the center and sides of the display, fold the side tabs in toward the front of the display. **Note**: They will NOT meet at the center.

The bottom tab is the anchor tab. Fold it toward the back of the display. Center the anchor tab in the heading section of a notebook page and glue it in place. The writing and drawing will NOT be visible when the anchor tab is glued in place. When the glue is dry, stand the display up so that the center section faces the page and the anchor is hidden to the back. Information will be visible when the display is standing at the top of a notebook page.

Note: Placement at the top of the page provides more writing surface onthe remainder of the flat page.

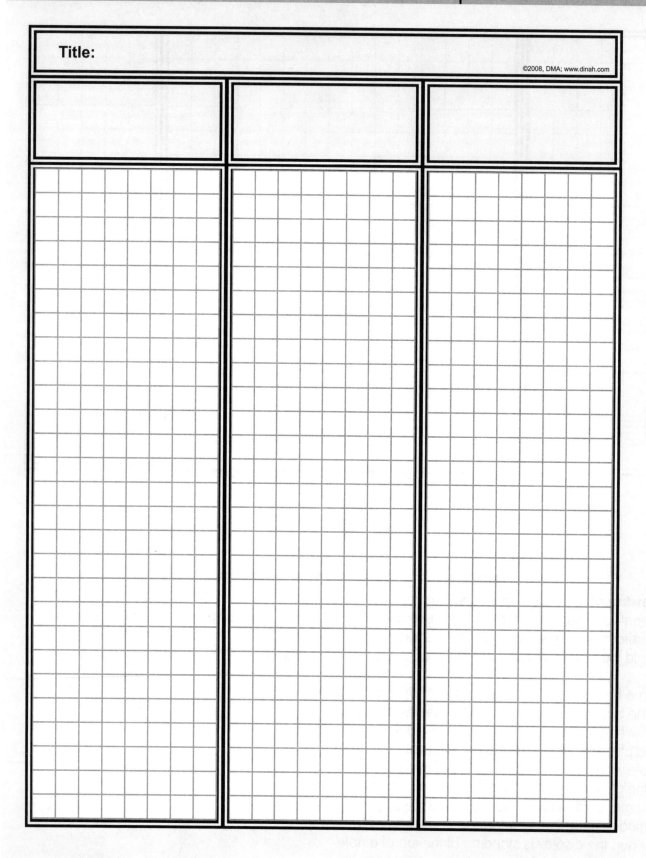

Title:

©2008, DMA; www.dinah.com

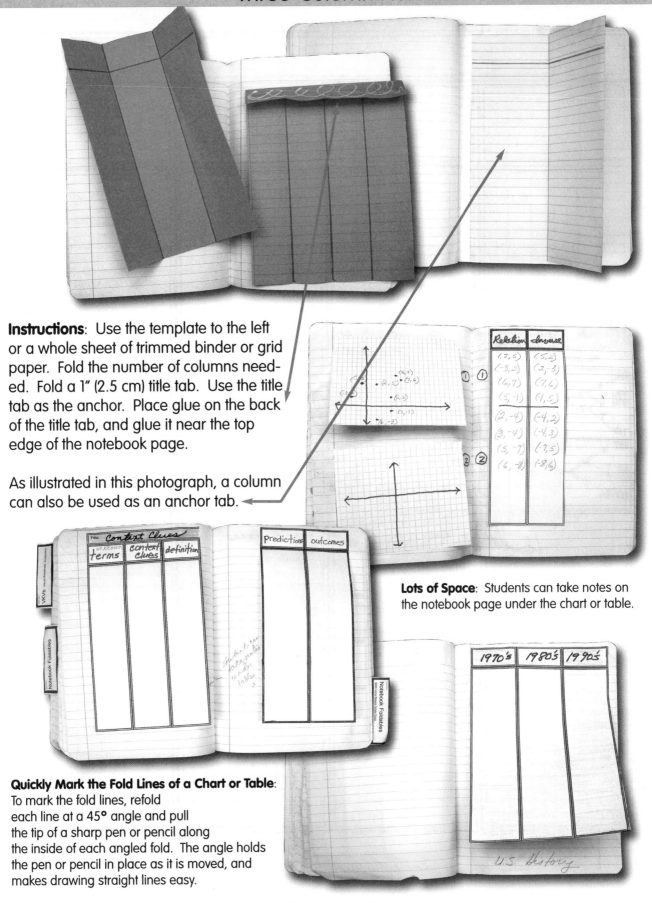

Instructions: Use the template to the left or a whole sheet of trimmed binder or grid paper. Fold the number of columns needed. Fold a 1" (2.5 cm) title tab. Use the title tab as the anchor. Place glue on the back of the title tab, and glue it near the top edge of the notebook page.

As illustrated in this photograph, a column can also be used as an anchor tab.

Lots of Space: Students can take notes on the notebook page under the chart or table.

Quickly Mark the Fold Lines of a Chart or Table: To mark the fold lines, refold each line at a 45° angle and pull the tip of a sharp pen or pencil along the inside of each angled fold. The angle holds the pen or pencil in place as it is moved, and makes drawing straight lines easy.

Four-Column Notebook Foldable® Chart Template

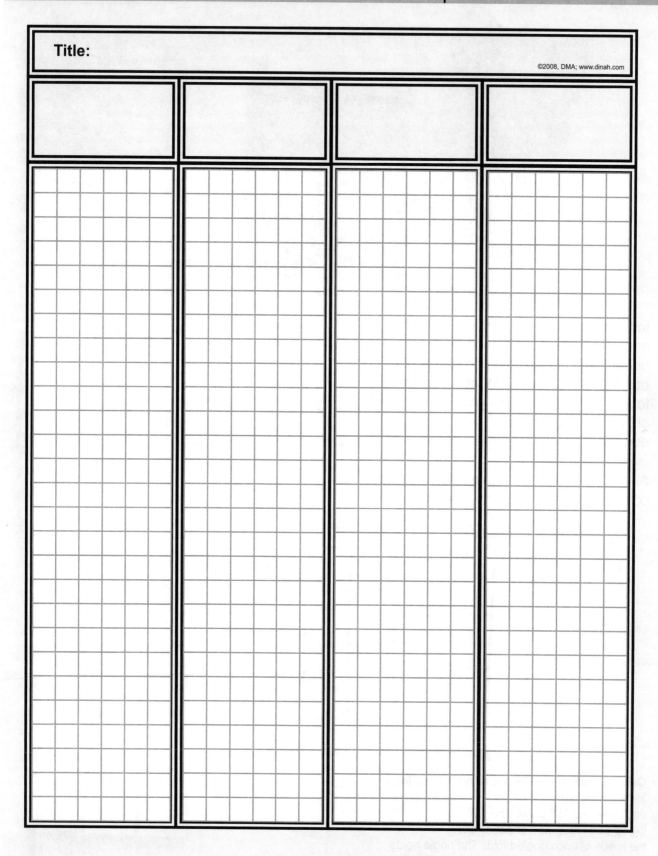

Title:

©2008, DMA; www.dinah.com

Instructions: See page 77 for folding instructions.

What Goes On and Under the Tabs?
Use the chart for any of the following:
- major chapter headings, key figures, dates, events, more
- see lists in *Dinah Zike's Big Book* series for content-specific ideas (See page 10)

In the columns or rows, have students write any of the following: main and/or supporting ideas, descriptions, definitions, explanations, calculations, questions, opinions, examples, diagrams, quotes, research information, summaries, other responses.

Make Notebook Foldable Charts Using any of the Following:
- whole or half-sheets of trimmed binder paper
- half-sheets of grid or photocopy paper
- large index cards
- sheets of steno paper or writing tablet paper
- whole sheet of small legal pad paper

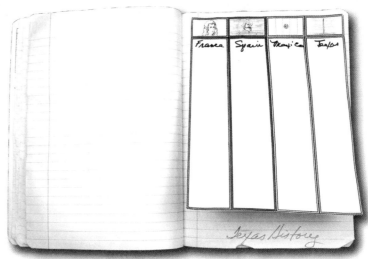

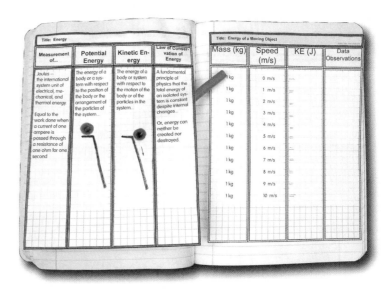

Title:

©2008, DMA; www.dinah.com

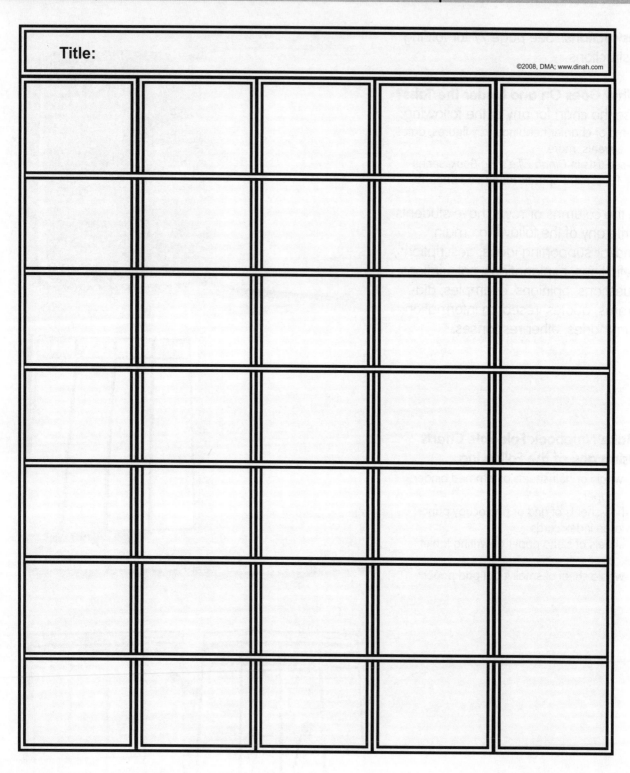

Instructions:

Use the template to the left or trimmed paper and fold the number of columns and rows needed. Always add one extra column and one extra row for labeling the columns and rows of a table or graph.

To mark the fold lines, refold each line at a 45° angle and pull the tip of a pen or pencil along the inside of the folds (See page 77). Use one of the title tabs as the anchor tab. Glue the anchor tab along the top edge of a page or along one of the side edges.

Instructions for Using the Template:

Cut the number of columns and rows needed. Remember to add one extra column and one extra row for labeling. Use either the vertical or horizontal title tab as the anchor tab. Glue the anchor tab onto a page in a notebook.

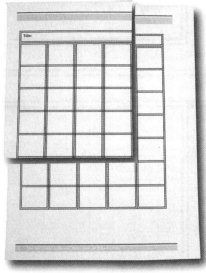

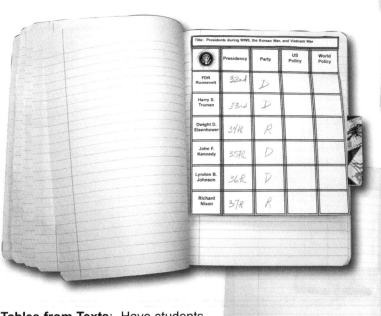

Tables from Texts: Have students make their own tables reflecting data found in their textbooks or on the internet.

Instructions: Use the templates in this book or half sheets of trimmed binder paper. One or more pockets can be glued onto a notebook page. The pockets to the right are glued on a vertical axis.

When gluing multiple pockets, begin with the bottom pocket and glue it so the top edge of the pocket aligns with the margin. Continue to glue pockets on top of this pocket, spacing them about ½" to ¾" apart. Label the pockets.

What Goes On and In the Pockets?

Use quarter or eighth sheets of binder paper or half sections of index cards in the pockets. On these cards students describe, define, explain, justify, diagram, prove, give examples, list supporting facts, summarize, question, and give other responses.

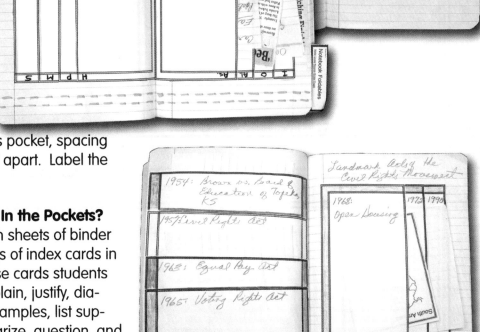

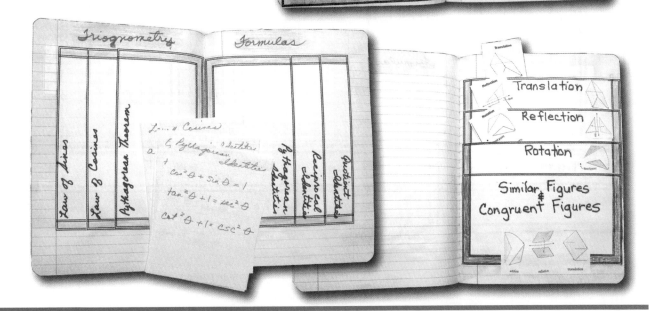

©2008, DMA; www.dinah.com

Title:

©2008, DMA; www.dinah.com

Title:

Instructions: Use the templates in this book or a half sheet of trimmed paper to make a horizontal pocket . Place glue around three sides of the pocket -- one long side and two short sides. Position the pocket towards the bottom of a page within a notebook, and glue the pocket in place so that the unglued, open end is pointing up. This open end will form the pocket.

What Goes In The Pocket?

Folded worksheets, information sheets, note cards, vocabulary terms recorded on quarter sheets of paper, index cards, publishing center graphics, folded worksheets or information sheets, and more can be stored in pockets.

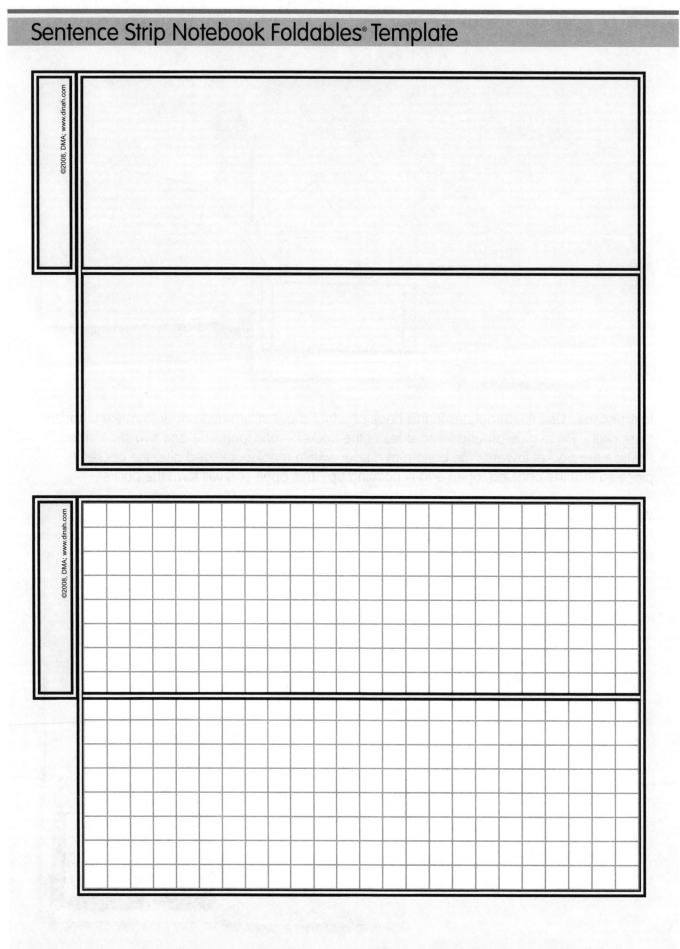

©2008, DMA; www.dinah.com

©2008, DMA; www.dinah.com

Instructions: Use the templates to the left or use a half sheet of trimmed binder paper for each sentence strip needed. Fold the strips in half on the long axis, like a hotdog. With the mountain of the fold up, cut a tab ½" from the left edge of the top section only.

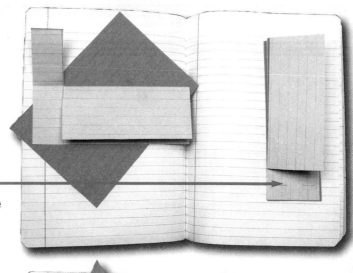

Following the steps above, make the needed number of sections. Staple and/or glue them together in the middle of the small left tabs.

For stability, glue the entire back of the last section into the notebook. Since this is a multi-sectioned Notebook Foldable, it needs extra support.

What Goes On and Under the Tabs?
Write lesson titles, questions, main ideas, key terms, etc., on the front tabs.

Respond to what is on the front tab by writing notes, definitions, thoughts, summaries, and more under the tabs.

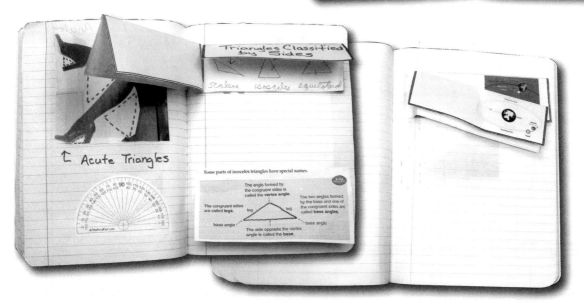

Title:

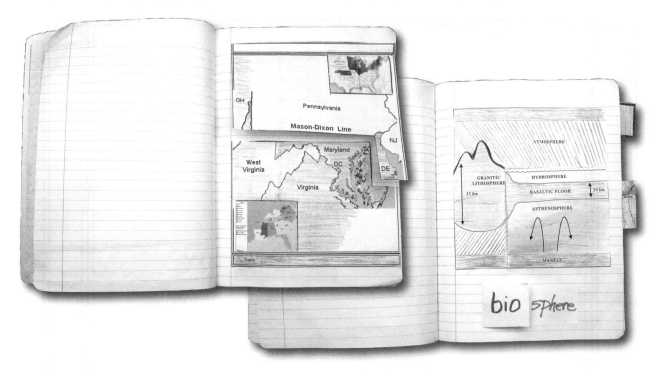

Instructions: This Notebook Foldable is used with a magazine picture, computer-generated diagram, student-drawn graphics, or graphics from a worksheet. Size the selected graphic to fit on a page within the type of notebook being used. Fold an anchor tab along the top and bottom edges of the selected graphic. Glue the anchor tabs onto a page in a notebook. When the glue is dry, cut the paper in half from left to right to illustrate information presented. See specific examples below.

What Goes On and Under the Tabs?

Place the following on the front tabs of the horizontal-cut Notebook Foldable:
-pictures or diagrams of things above and below:
    plants above and below ground
    lava and magma
    composition of Earth above and below the crust
-political divisions:
    the Mason-Dixon Line
    border between North and South Dakota
-geographic features, borders, or boundaries
    USA and Canadian border

Under the tabs, have students write any of the following: main and/or supporting ideas, descriptions, definitions, explanations, calculations, questions, opinions, examples, diagrams, quotes, research information, summaries, outlines, other responses.

Cut along the topography of the land to illustrate magma (below) and lava (above).

©2008, DMA; www.dinah.com

Title:

Instructions: This Notebook Foldable is used with a magazine picture, computer-generated diagram, student-drawn graphics, or graphics from a worksheet. Size the selected graphic to fit on a page within the type of notebook being used. Fold an anchor tab along the left and right edges of the selected graphic. Glue the anchor tabs onto a page in a notebook. When the glue is dry, cut the paper in half from top to bottom to illustrate information presented.

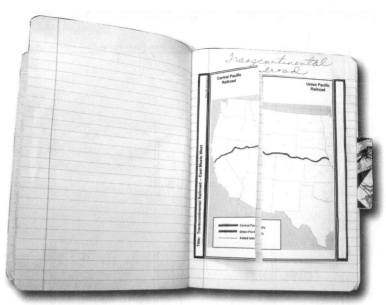

What Goes On and Under the Tabs?
Place any of the following on the front tab of the vertical-cut Notebook Foldable:
- pictures or diagrams of things divided by East and West
    - Transcontinental Railroad
    - border between Virginia and West Virginia
- pictures or diagrams of things divided by left and right
    - positive and negative integers left and right of zero
- political divisions
    - history of East and West Germany and the Berlin Wall
- geographic features, borders, or boundaries
    - Ural Mountains as part of the boundary between Europe and Asia

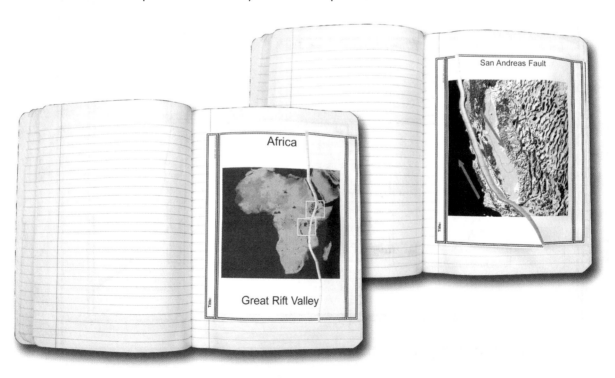

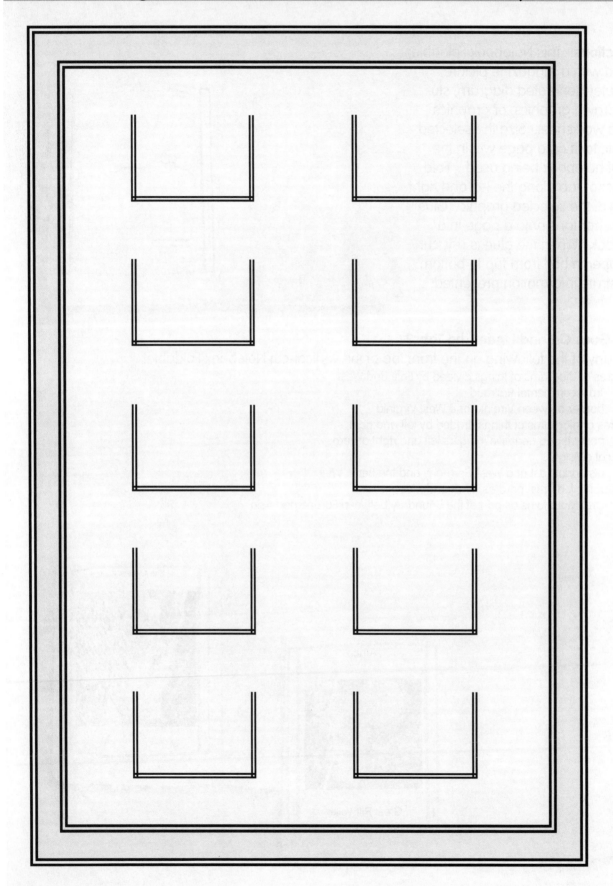

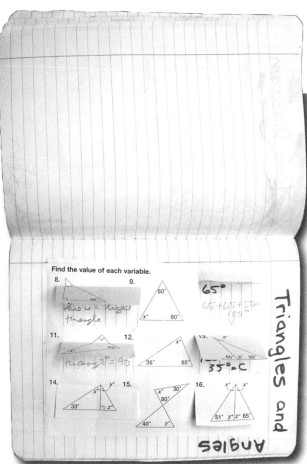

Instructions for Using a Picture or Diagram:

This Notebook Foldable is used with a magazine picture, computer-generated diagram, student-drawn graphics, or graphics from a worksheet. The example on the left is from a math worksheet. Size the selected graphic to fit on a page within the type of notebook being used. Gently crease the picture or diagram in half at points where tabs are desired. Cut in from the fold line half of the desired length of the tab. Turn scissors and cut up the height of the desired tab. Open to find a tab within the picture on top of a section of the picture or diagram that is to be featured.

Instructions for Using Templates:

Students can draw a picture or diagram on the template on page 90 before it is cut.

What Goes On and Under the Tabs?

Usually the picture or diagram on top of the tab is the "label," and students respond to that material by writing under the tabs.

Right: Pictures that are public domain can be copied and used within composition books.

Copies of student- or teacher-generated photographs with tabs also make interesting notebook additions.

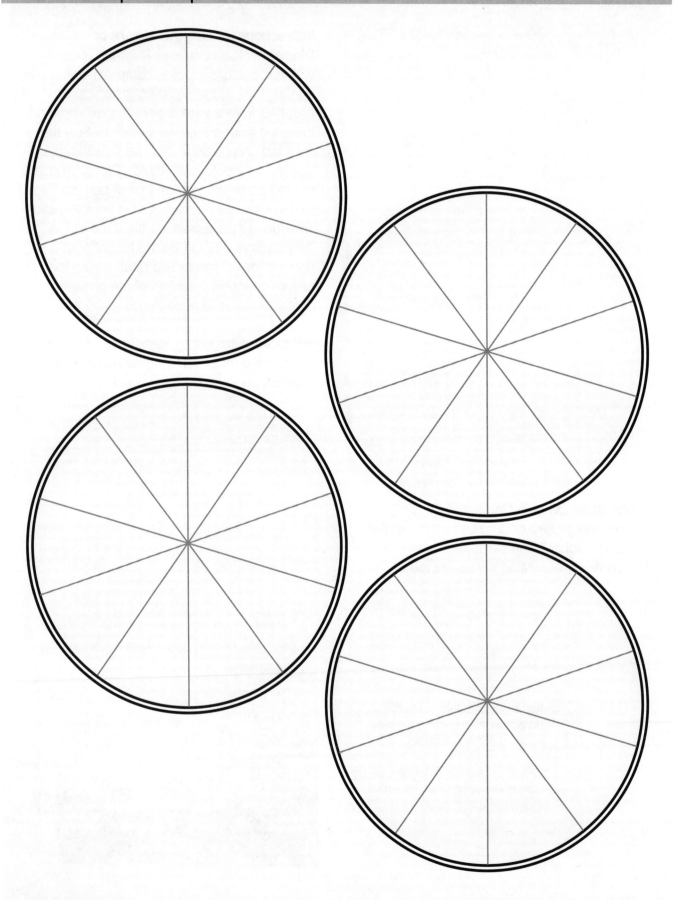

What Goes On and Under the Tabs?

Statistics presented as percentages can be found in all content subject units, themes, and textbooks. Adding circle graphs to notebooks places a focus on important data that can be illustrated by percentages. Percentages compare quantities to other quantities. For example, if 70.8% of Earth's surface is water, then 29.2% is land. Circle graph quantities can be used to explain cause-and-effect relationships, rates of increase and/or decrease, and similarities and differences between two things.

Circle graphs can be glued flat into student notebooks, or they can be folded in half with only half of the circle glued to form a half-circle tab.

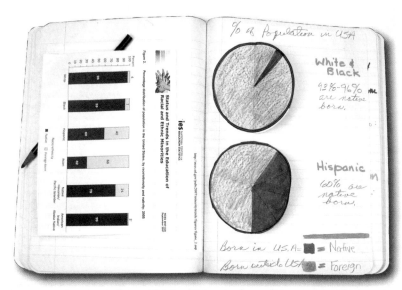

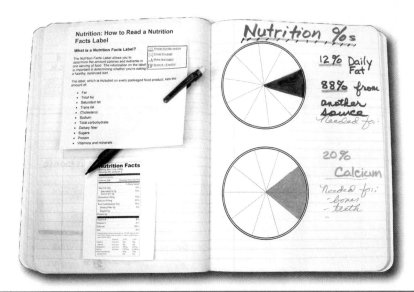

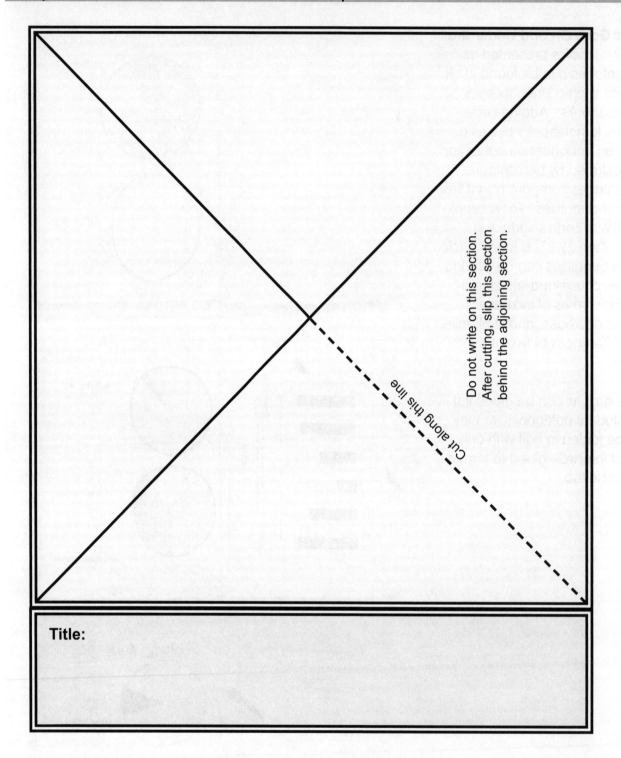

Do not write on this section.
After cutting, slip this section behind the adjoining section.

Cut along this line

Title:

What Goes On and Under the Tabs?

Write the following on the front tabs of Pyramid Notebook Foldables:

- -three main ideas or categories --
  water cycle: evaporation, condensation, precipitation
- -three skills being studied -- *-ed, -ing, -ly*
- -three key terms --
  rotation, tessalation, reflection
- -names of three people, places, things
- -**K**now, **W**hat to know, **L**earned
- -see lists in *Dinah Zike's Big Book* series for content-specific ideas (See page 10)

Behind the tabs to the inside of the pyramid, have students describe, define, explain, justify, diagram, prove, give examples, list supporting facts, and more.

Pyramid Diorama: Stand the pyramid on one side to make a diorama. A physical object might be placed in the diorama for observation while students write in their notebooks.

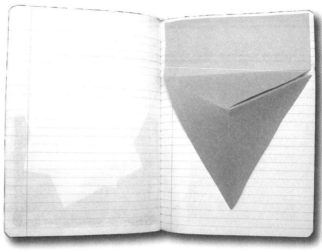

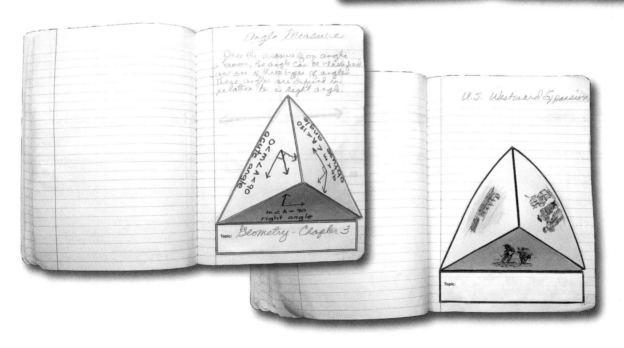

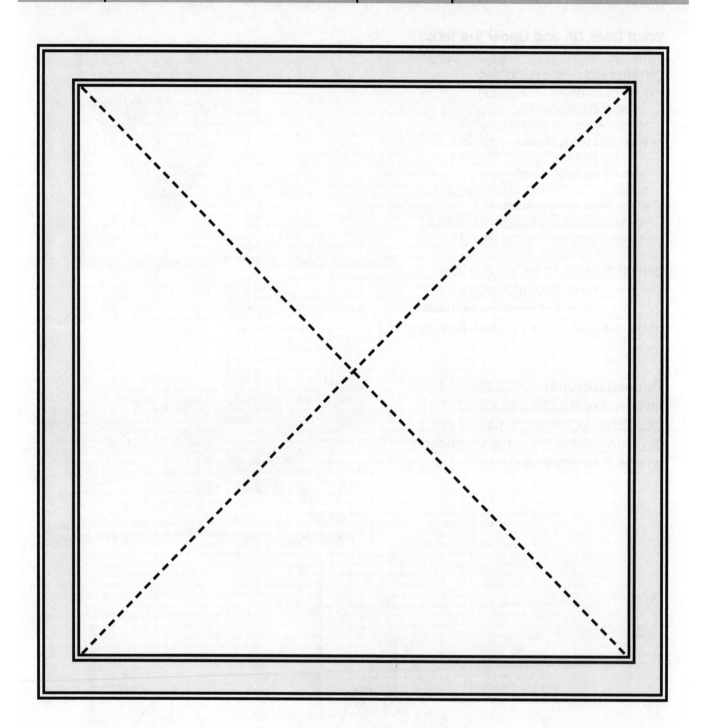

What Goes On and Under the Tabs?

Write the following on the front tabs of Envelope Notebook Foldables:

- -four main ideas or categories
- -four skills being studied
- -four key terms
- -four steps
- -names of four people, places, things
- -**K**now, **W**ant to know, **L**earned, **H**ow it will be used
- -see lists in *Dinah Zike's Big Book* series for content-specific ideas (See page 10)

Under the tabs, have students write any of the following: main and/or supporting ideas, descriptions, definitions, explanations, calculations, questions, opinions, examples, diagrams, quotes, research information, summaries, outlines, other responses.

Four-Step Cycles: Use this Notebook Foldable to illustrate cycles like the one to the right illustrating market supply and demand.

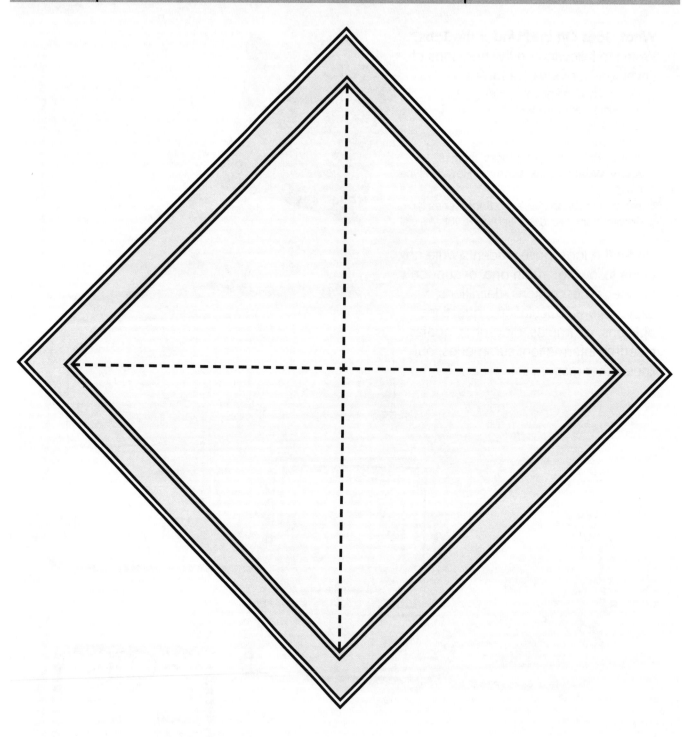

What Goes On and Under the Tabs?

Write the following on the front tabs of the Envelope Notebook Foldable:

- Four main ideas or categories
  Example: perpendicular lines
  four 90° angles = 360°
- Four skills being studied
- Four key terms
- Four steps
- Names of four people, places, things
- **W**ho? **W**hat? **W**hen? and **W**here?
- **K**now, **W**ant to know, **L**earned, **H**ow it will be used
- See lists in *Dinah Zike's Big Book* series for content-specific ideas (See page 10)

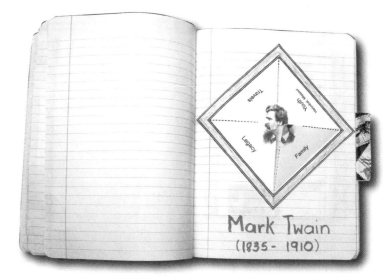

Under the tabs, have students write any of the following: main and/or supporting ideas, descriptions, definitions, explanations, summaries, other responses.

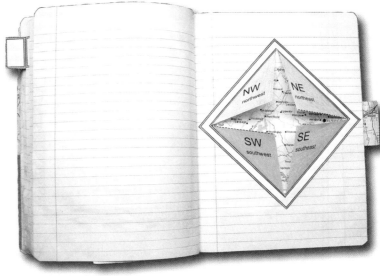

Instructions:

Fold a square in half to form two crossing diagonal fold lines.

With the paper folded along one of these fold lines, cut in from the fold along the perpendicular fold, stopping ½" from the point. (The other cut will be made later.)

Place glue around the four outer edges of the Foldable and glue it on a notebook page. After the glue has dried, cut along the inner fold lines to form four-right triangle tabs.

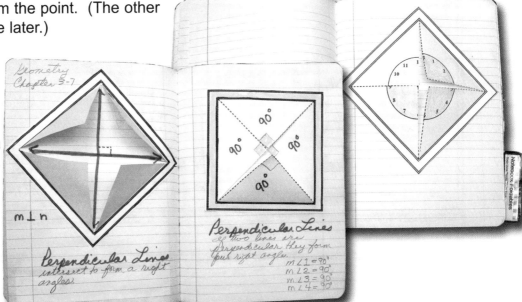

Title:

Cube Project Notebook Foldable®

When to Glue:
Glue the cube project into the notebook **after** students have finished labeling, writing, and/or drawing on the sides.

Instructions Using Binder Paper:
Use two trimmed sheets of binder paper. See page 18.

Stack the two sheets of paper and fold them in half along the short axis so that one side of both sheets is ½" longer. Fold this ½" strip over the short sides to form ½" tabs. Separate the two sheets.

On one of the folded papers, place a small amount of glue along the small folded tab, next to the valley but not in it.

Place the non-folded (straight) edge of the second sheet of paper square into the valley and fold the glue-covered tab over this sheet of paper. Press flat until the glue holds.

Repeat with the other side.

Allow the glue to dry completely, and then trim ½" to 1" off three of the bottom edges. The remaining tab forms an anchor tab.

Fold this anchor tab back and forth to form a hinge. With the cube open, glue the anchor tab along the center top edge or bottom edge of a notebook page.

After the glue has dried, the cube can be collapsed flat for storage.

Note: It is easier to write on the cube after it is glued into the notebook if it is glued to the bottom of a page and folded upward for storage.

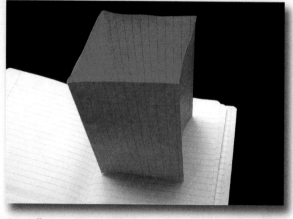

Standing Cube Foldable

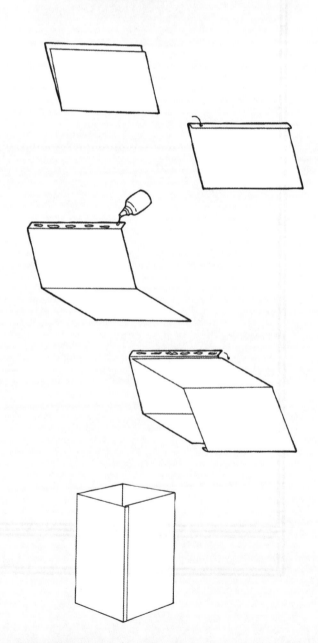

Instructions Using Templates:

Photocopy the two sections on pages 102-103, or print the pages from the Notebook Foldable CD. Fold each sheet in half, leaving a ½" strip along one side. Fold the ½" strip forward over the short edge.

Stand the L-shaped sections on end so that the straight edges align in valley folds to form a standing cube.

Glue one of the ½" strips over the straight edges to secure the shape. Note that it is easier to lay the cube on its side before gluing.

Fold the anchor tab back and away from the cube. Use the anchor tab to secure the cube. (See instructions on the previous page and photos on this page)

What Goes On the Sides?

Write the following on the four sides of the Cube Project Notebook Foldable:
- four main ideas or categories
- four skills being studied
- four key terms
- four steps
- names of four people, places, things
- **W**ho? **W**hat? **W**hen? **W**here?
- **K**now, **W**ant to know, **L**earned, **H**ow it will be used
- see lists in *Dinah Zike's Big Book* series for content-specific ideas (See page 10)

Under the tabs, have students write any of the following: main and/or supporting ideas, descriptions, definitions, explanations, calculations, questions, opinions, examples, diagrams, quotes, research information, summaries, outlines, other responses.

Anchor Tab

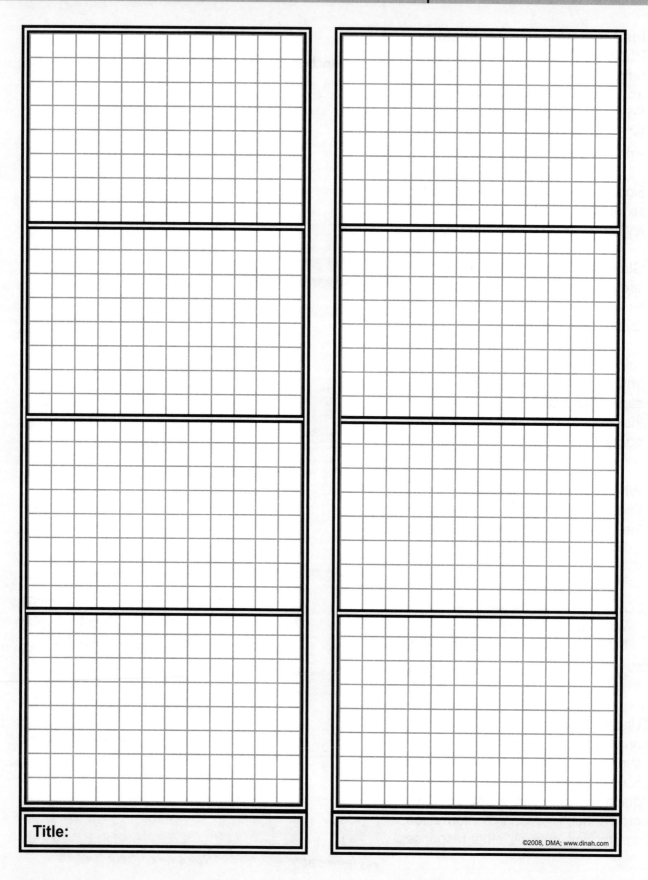

Title:

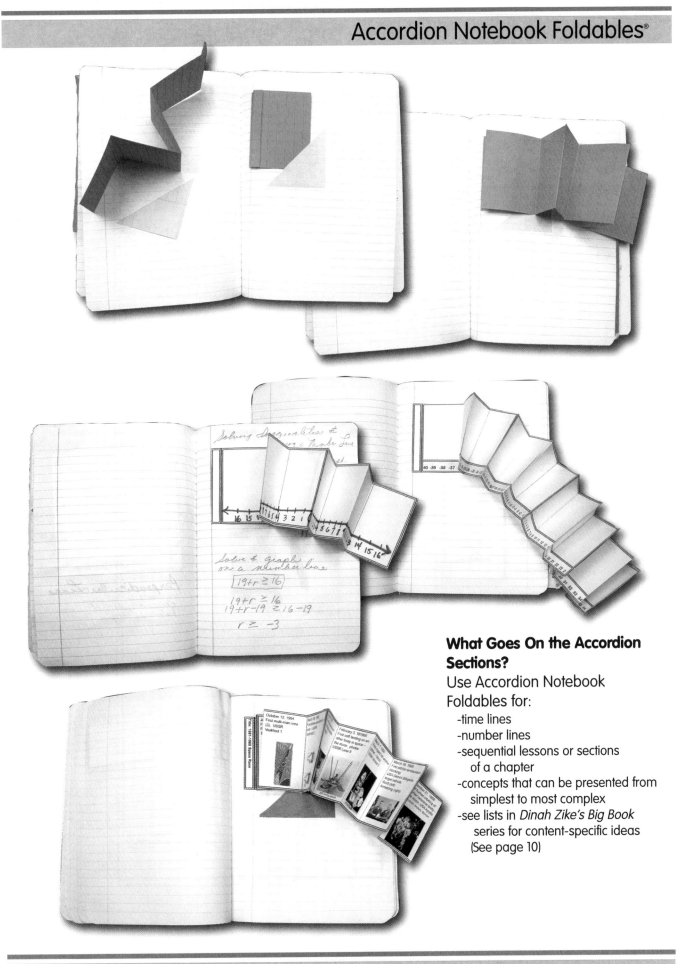

What Goes On the Accordion Sections?

Use Accordion Notebook Foldables for:

- -time lines
- -number lines
- -sequential lessons or sections of a chapter
- -concepts that can be presented from simplest to most complex
- -see lists in *Dinah Zike's Big Book* series for content-specific ideas (See page 10)

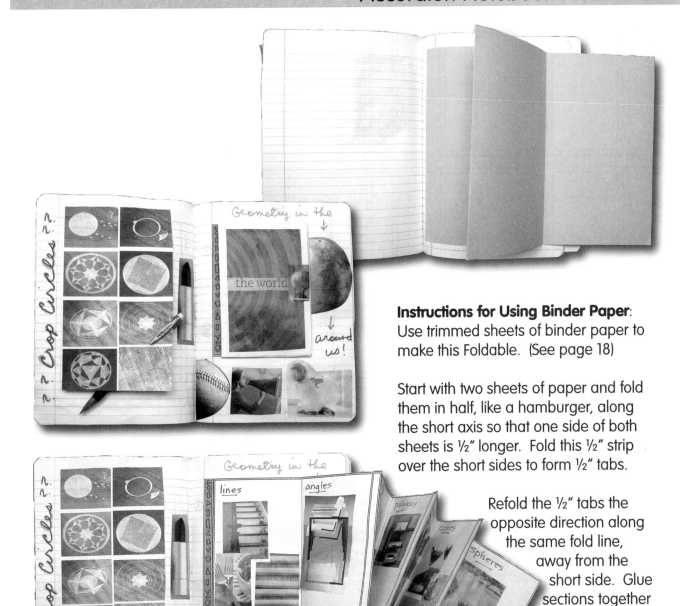

Instructions for Using Binder Paper:
Use trimmed sheets of binder paper to make this Foldable. (See page 18)

Start with two sheets of paper and fold them in half, like a hamburger, along the short axis so that one side of both sheets is ½" longer. Fold this ½" strip over the short sides to form ½" tabs.

Refold the ½" tabs the opposite direction along the same fold line, away from the short side. Glue sections together to form an accordion by gluing a straight edge of one section into the valley of the other section.

Use the remaining ½" tab as an anchor tab. Glue the accordion onto a notebook page.

Using the Templates to the Left to Make Tabs:
Determine the number and location of all tabs. Mark the locations using scratch paper or sticky notes.

Cut out the number of tabs needed and fold them in half.

With the "mountain" (top of the fold) up, write titles on the front and back of all label tabs. This positioning will ensure the writing on the tabs is aligned correctly after gluing.

Place a small amount of glue on the back of both sides of each tab.

Place the tab over the outer right edge of a divider page so that the edge of the page is captured between the bottom sections of the tab.

Allow glue to dry completely before closing the notebook.

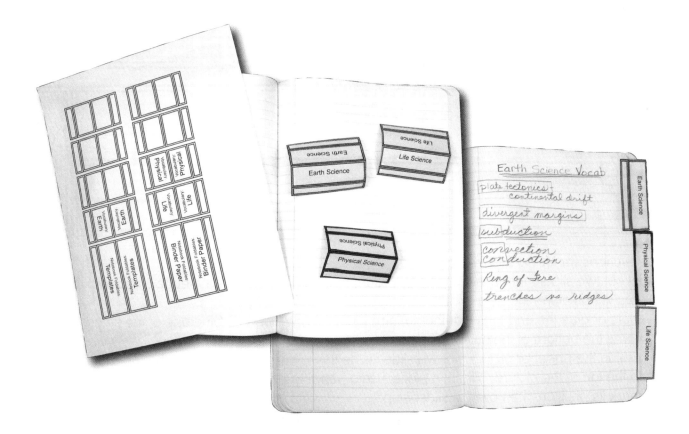

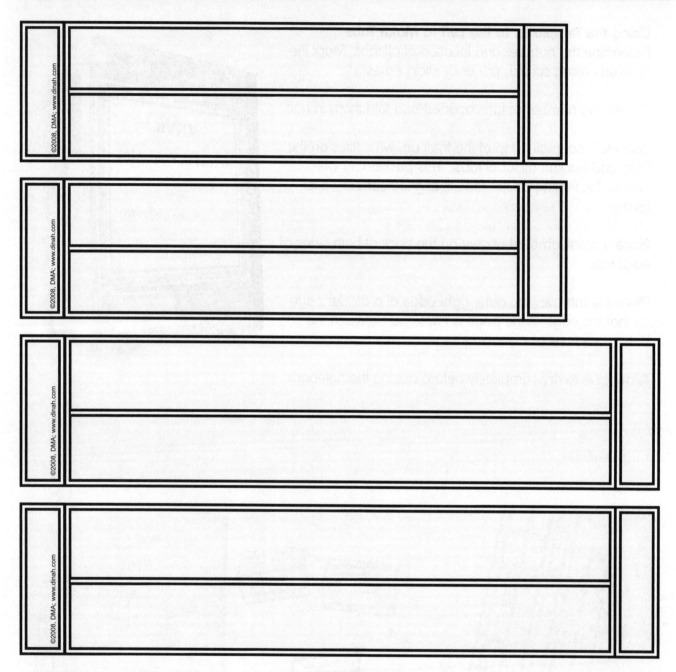

Instructions for Using Sliders:

- Cut out two sliders for each diagram or picture to be placed within a notebook, and fold the sliders in half along the long axis.
- Staple or glue the end tabs together to form long, narrow pockets. Glue one of the strips towards the bottom of the notebook page.
- Position the paper or picture that will slide inside this lower slider strip. Slip the top slider strip onto the top of the picture. When in place, use a pencil to trace around the top of the slider strip to mark its position. Remove the slider strip.
- Place glue on the back of the strip and glue in place, using the pencil line as a guide. Glue the strip about 1/8" above the top of the pencil line to allow room for the picture to slide. Slip the items inside the top and bottom slider strips and move the picture.

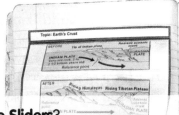

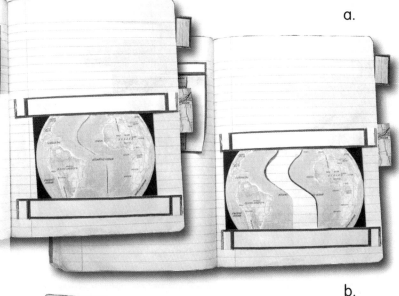

a.

What are Sliders?

Sliders are shallow pockets that hold strips of paper or sections of a diagram along either the top and bottom or the left and right sides. The sliders allow the featured sections to be moved together or apart.

Example: Sliders are perfect for illustrating plate tectonics:

a. A single set of sliders -- one top and one bottom -- was used to show the Atlantic as an expanding ocean due to magma welling up at the Mid-Atlantic Ridge (expanding approximately 1" (2.5 cm) per year).

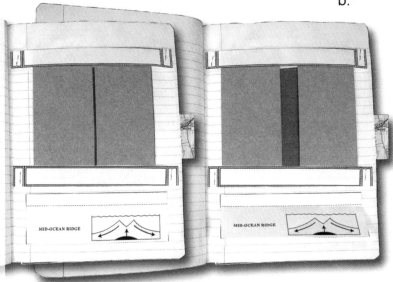

b.

b. These sliders are the same as those described above; however, a piece of red paper was glued on the notebook page between the sliders. The two blue sections were slipped into the sliders. As the blue sections are moved apart, the exposed red represents the magma welling up between two tectonic plates.

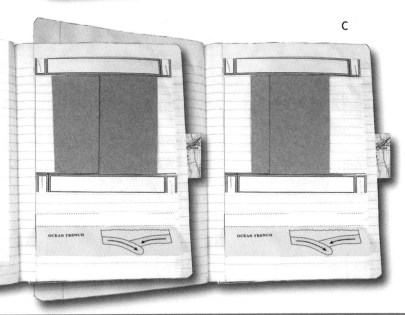

c

c. To show objects moving toward and over or under each other, two sliders are used at both the top and the bottom. The sliders are folded and glued together (or stapled on the ends). Position the paper within the sliders before gluing to ensure that it will stay within the sliders after they are glued.

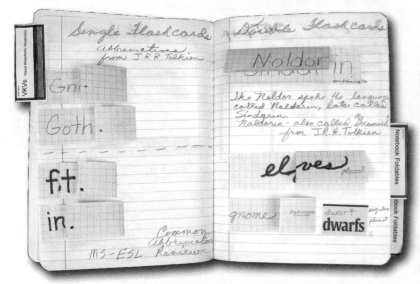

Using Real World Print (RWP):

Vocabulary words and titles found in magazines and newspapers (or any form of real world print) can be glued into notebooks.

Instructions for Using VKVs (Visual Kinesthetic Vocabulary) in Notebooks:

When making VKVs for notebooks, use quarter sheets of binder or grid paper. This size will allow multiple VKVs to be placed on the same page, or to allow a VKV to be placed above or below tabbed Notebook Foldables.

More About Dinah Zike's Visual Kinesthetic Vocabulary:

Dinah has designed over twenty-five folds to make vocabulary terms kinesthetic. The instructions for these folds and information on how they are used are featured in Dinah's Foldables and VKVs series, each of which are over 200 pages in length. These books are filled with over 1,000 photographs that simplify folding while stimulating ideas for use. The books contain great vocabulary builders for all students, including those in ESL, ELL, and ESOL programs.

Investigate the Following for More Information on VKVs (Visual Kinesthetic Vocabulary):

Dinah Zike's Foldables® and VKVs™ for PreK-2nd Grades:
Phonics, Spelling, Vocabulary --Now Available for Ordering

Dinah Zike's Foldables® and VKVs™ for 3rd-6th Grades:
Spelling, Vocabulary , and Phonics Review -- Available September 2008

Dinah Zike's Foldables® and VKVs™ for 6th-12th Grades:
Spelling, Vocabulary, and Test Prep -- Available 2009

VKV Examples (right): Each VKV flash-card make from two to 16 words or phrases by moving tabs that change parts of the word (prefix, suffix, root, other) or phrase.

army of soldiers
ants
frogs

take a bath
break
walk

catch a cold
plane
ball

make time
space
over

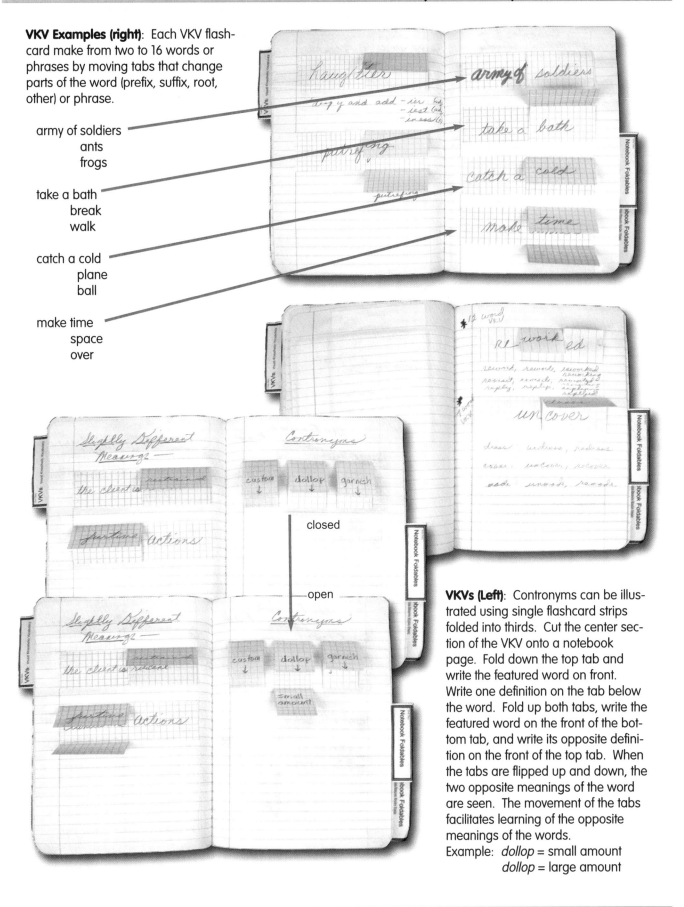

closed

open

VKVs (Left): Contronyms can be illustrated using single flashcard strips folded into thirds. Cut the center section of the VKV onto a notebook page. Fold down the top tab and write the featured word on front. Write one definition on the tab below the word. Fold up both tabs, write the featured word on the front of the bottom tab, and write its opposite definition on the front of the bottom tab, and write its opposite definition on the front of the top tab. When the tabs are flipped up and down, the two opposite meanings of the word are seen. The movement of the tabs facilitates learning of the opposite meanings of the words.
Example: *dollop* = small amount
            dollop = large amount

Clear Tape Laminate: As illustrated in the photos on this page, 2" clear tape can be used to laminate objects onto the following:
- flashcards
- quarter sheets of paper
- index cards
- a page in a notebook

A computer disk sleeve can be used used to store quarter-sheet specimen cards.

Use clear tape to laminate the following:
- leaves, flowers, roots
- insect body parts
- soil samples
- seeds
- coins
- stamps
- pictures
- autographs, more.

Coin Holders: Cardboard coin holders with clear acetate windows can be used to make slides for viewing specimens. These slides can be stored within a notebook by placing them within small pockets made using 2½″ x 4¼″ manila envelopes. (See pages 29 to 31 for information on using envelopes in notebooks)

Right and Below: A quarter-sized coin holder can be used to view a specimen under a microscope. Open the coin holder and place the specimen in the center of the acetate window. Fold the holder in half to cover the specimen. Use three small pieces of clear tape, one on each of the open sides, to seal the specimen within the holder. Store the specimen in small pockets within a notebook as illustrated on the previous page.

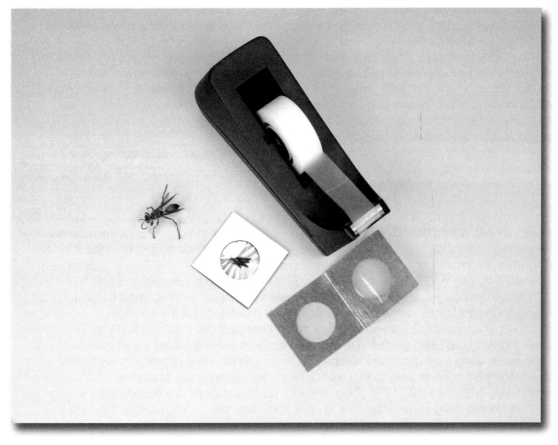

Evidence-Based Resources to Support 12 Common Instructional Skills & Tools Used with Foldables® and VKVs™

Cause and Effect

- Williams, J. P.; Nubla-Kung, A.M; Pollini, S.; Stafford, K. B.; Garcia, A.; Snyder, A. E. 2007. Teaching cause-effect text structure through social studies content to at-risk second graders. *Journal of Learning Disabilities*, 40. 111-120.
- "Cause & Effect." www.literacymatters.org/content/text/cause.htm
- "Cause and Effect Reading Lesson Plan." An introduction for science teachers to the concept of cause & effect. Offers a chart, chain of events, problem/solution diagram, and Venn diagram to analyze different aspects of cause and effect. www.everestquest.com/read2.htm

Compare and Contrast

- Hall, K.M.; Sabey, B. L.; and McClessan, M. 2005. Expository text comprehension: helping primary-grade teachers use expository texts to full advantage. *Reading Psychology*, 26. 211-234.
- Marzano, R.J.; Pickering, D.J.; and Pollock., J.E. 2001. Classroom Instruction That Works. Identifying similarities & differences is the #1 way to raise student achievement. Representing similarities & differences in graphic or symbolic form enhances learners' understanding of and ability to use knowledge.
- Chen, 1999; Cole & McLeod, 1999; Glynn & Takahashi, 1998, Lin, 1996. Combining the instructional strategies of asking students to construct their own means for comparing similarities and differences with the use of nonlinguistic representation significantly enhances student achievement.

Concept Maps & Webs

- Horten et al. 1993. Meta-analysis of studies using concept mapping as a learning strategy showed that concept mapping raised student achievement on average 0.46 standard deviations and contributed to strong improvement in student attitude.
- Novak & Gowan. 1984. In addition to a key role as assessment tools (consider differences before, during and after instruction), concept maps offer a useful way to help students learn how to learn.
- Readence, J. E., Moore, D. W., and Rickelman, R. J. 2000. Pre-reading Activities for Content Area Reading and Learning. 62-81. Describes seven graphic representation strategies.
- Constructing concept maps is a demanding cognitive task that requires training. www.flaguide.org/cat/minutepapers/conmap4.php
- Concept maps, used for over 25 years, help students focus on the "big picture," enabling them to devote more time to conceptual understanding versus rote learning. www.flaguide.org/cat/minutepapers/conmap7.php

Graphs and Diagrams

- Disess, Hammer, Sherin & Kopakowski. 1991. One of the difficulties with conventional instruction is that students' meta-knowledge is often not engaged, so they come to know "how to graph" without understanding what graphs are for or why the conventions make sense.
- Friel, S.N, Curcio, F.R, Bright, G. W. 2001. *Journal for Research in Math. Education*, 32, 2, 124-158. Four critical factors influence graph comprehension: purposes for using graphs, task characteristics (visual decoding, judgment, tasks, and the context or semantic content of a graph), discipline characteristics, and reader characteristics . . . Graph sense or comprehension develops gradually as one creates graphs and uses already-designed graphs in a variety of problem-solving contexts that involve the use of data" . . . Consider using a constructivist perspective to enable students to organize and make sense of information before introducing formal work with the traditional types of graphs.
- Pressley. et. al, 1988; Woloshy et al., 1990. Non-linguistic representations are important for engaging students in elaborative thinking in two ways. When students elaborate on knowledge, they not only understand it in greater depth, but also recall it much more easily.

Journaling and Bookmaking

- Fordham, N.W., Wellman, D. & Sandman, A. 2002. Taming the text. The Social Studies. 93. 149-158. Writing to learn in all content areas is vital, because considering a topic under study and then writing requires more extensive processing than reading alone entails.
- NWP & Nagin. 2003. Writing to Learn (WTL) advocates encouraging writing to help students discover new knowledge--to sort through previous understandings, draw connections, and uncover new ideas as they write. WTL activities can also encourage reflection on learning strategies and thereby increase students' meta-cognitive skills. (exs: journals, learning logs, exit slips)
- Sprenger, M. 2005. Students reinforce their learning when they communicate and especially write about "their content, be it concepts, facts or procedures."

KWL and Variations

- Eshelman, John W., Ed.D. 2001. Commentary on Behavior and Instruction: Ausubel, Advance Organizers, and Replicable Research. www.members.aol.com;johneshleman/comment12.html
- Frey, N. and Fisher, D.B. 2006. 19-20. *Language Arts Workshop: Purposeful Reading and Writing Instruction.*
- Merkley, D.M. and Jeffries, D. 2001. Guidelines for Implementing a Graphic Organizer. *The Reading Teacher* 54 (4), 538-540.
- Ogle, D. M. *The Reading Teacher*, 39, 564-570. KWL: A teaching model developed by Ogle in 1986 that develops active reading of expository text.
- Readence, J.E., Bean, T.W., & Baldwin, R. S. 1998. Teachers can vary the way to expose students to information before they "learn" it. KWL is a good, logical graphic application.

Main Idea & Supportive Facts

- Barton, J. and Sawyer, D. 2004. Our students are ready for this: Comprehension instruction in the elementary school. *The Reading Teacher*, 57, 334-347.
- Just, M. and Carpenter, P. 1992. A capacity theory of comprehension: Individual differences in working memory. *Psychological Review*, 1992, 122-149. In most reading situations we read for the main points, in part, due to memory constraints. We can't process every line in the text at the same level if our working memory is overloaded with too much information. Part of the information then is displaced or 'forgotten.'
- Tomitch. L.M.B. 2000. Teaching main ideas -- Are we really teaching? *Linguagem & Ensino*, 45-53. Main idea identification is one of the most important literacy comprehension skills. Textbooks typically provide tasks or practice involving the main ideas, but do not actually provide explicit procedures and instruction in main idea identification and formulation.

Opposites (Pairing of Antonyms)

- Heidenheimer, P. 1978. Logical relations in the semantic processing of children between six and ten: emergence of antonym and synonym categorization. *Child Development*. 49. 1243-1246.
- Jones, Steven. 2007. "Opposites" in discourse: a comparison on antonym use across four domains. *Journal of Pragmatics*. 39. 1105-1119.
- Jones, S. and Murphy, M. L. Antonymy in childhood: a corpus-based approach to acquisition.
- McKeown,M. G. 1993. Creating effective definitions for young word learners. *Reading Research Quarterly*, 27, 16-31.

Questioning

- Cotton, K. Teaching questioning skills: Franklin Elementary School. *School Improvement Research Series*. http://www.nwrel.org/scpd/sirs/4/snap13.html. Research on questioning reveals among other findings that teaching students how to respond to and how to frame higher-level questions is positively related to their voluntary participation in such higher cognitive processes in classroom discussions.
- McKenzie, Jamie. 2005. Learning to Question to Wonder to Learn.
- Raphael, T. E., 1986. Promotes replacing traditional cognitive hierarchies of questions relative to text and graphics with classifications that identify the kinds of transactions that learners/readers use with the text to answer questions. One way to teach these important QAR strategies is with the help of graphic organizers.

Sequencing Events/Cycles/Ordering

- Cusimano, A., M.Ed. 2006. Auditory Sequential Memory Instructional Workbook. Within the area of the brain controlling the processing of information presented in isolation or sequential order, each aspect (numbers, letters and words) is specific unto itself. Students who have mastered the skill of number memory may not have developed the skill of remembering letters and words, or vice versa. Thus, we must consider the development of all numbers, letters, and words separately.
- Frey, N.and Fisher, D. B. 2006. 337-340. *Language Arts Workshop: Purposeful Reading and Writing Instruction.* Focus on temporal or sequential text structure and signal words in expository text with explicit instruction on structure and styles used in content area texts and informational trade books.

Tables and Charts

- Bruning, Schraw, Norby & Roning. 2003. Research on the effects of students self-generating material that involves recoding, as is built into interactive graphic organizers, shows that students consistently do better.
- Katayama & Robinson, 2000. Evidence suggests that blank or partially completed graphic organizers promote greater text comprehension than those completed in advance for students.
- Graphic displays outside of text, such as pictures, geographic and concept maps, tables and charts, and the like promote recall of text when used in concert with each other. The belief is that such displays are effective because they provide the learner with two avenues to memory: verbal (text) and spatial (the placement of information in relation to other facts), and that the spatial and verbal work in concert with one another (Kulhavy, Lee, & Caterino, 1985 as cited in Fischer et. al., 2007, *50 Content Area Strategies for Adolescent Literacy.* p. 3). "For real learning to occur, students must use the graphic organizer to transform information. The goal . . . is not to fill it out; that's a worksheet." The graphic organizer "is an external storage device for information" and to be useful, it "should be used to transform information into verbal or written form" so that students can make the information their own. Fischer et. al., 2007. *50 Content Area Strategies for Adolescent Literacy.* p. 3.

Vocabulary Development

- Baumann, F.F. and Kame'enui, E.J. 2004. *Vocabulary Instruction: Research to Practice.* Three of four research-based modes for teaching vocabulary: wide reading, explicit teaching of specific words, teaching of word-learning strategies, and development of word consciousness can be well supported by interactive graphic organizers. Marzano's vision for direct vocabulary instruction aims for a top-level linguistic understanding of words accompanied by visual representation of terms that students encounter in their academic reading.
- Beck, I. L, McKeown, M. G, & Kucan, L. 2002. *Bringing Words to Life: Robust Vocabulary Instruction.*
- Dolch, E. W. Problems in Reading, 1948. First publication of the Dolch high frequency list.
- Fry, E. B. 2004. The Vocabulary Teacher's Book of Lists.
- Fry, E. B. and Kress, J. E. 2006. The Reading Teacher's Book of Lists, 5th Edition.
- Moore, D. W. and Readence, J. 1984 . A qualitative and quantitative review of graphic organizer research. Journal of Educational Research. 78. 11-17. Meta-analysis of 24 studies suggests that vocabulary knowledge gains following graphic organizer use may be even greater than comprehension gains.
- Sakiey, E. and Fry, E. B. 1979. 3000 Instant Words. Presents the 3,000 most frequently used words in rank and alphabetical orders. ERIC ID169516
- White T.G., Sowell, V., and Yanagihara, A. 1989. Teaching elementary students to use word-part clues. *The Reading Teacher.* 42. 302-309. Includes list of 20 most common prefixes and suffixes.

Dinah Zike Academy   dzacademy.com

Dinah Zike is proud to introduce the Dinah Zike Academy, a teacher training institute outside of San Antonio in the beautiful and historic Texas Hill Country.

Dinah: *It has always been my dream to have a location for teachers to immerse themselves in a fully developed, hands-on lab setting that will provide strategies to address diverse learners, meet state and national benchmarks, and build student learning skills for life. I also want to provide the opportunity for teachers to become Dinah Zike Certified trainers for their district, state, or nationwide, because I can't physically reach all the teachers who want to learn more about Foldables and my other teaching strategies.*

In three-day, jam-packed sessions at the Academy, Dinah and/or DZA's pro facilitators will engage and immerse you in the power and potential of 3-D interactive graphic organizers, dynamic and efficient classroom organization, and effective teaching strategies across age-grade levels and content areas. Research grounding, implementation for a variety of learners, and practicality are built in. A session maximum of 24 participants allows for hands-on individual and small-group work, technology use, and direct application to participants' teaching practices. Some seminars are cross-curricular and targeted to either elementary or secondary levels. Others are focused on specific content/subject areas, such as science, mathematics, social studies, and reading/language arts.

The expansive Academy is well-equipped with group and individual classrooms, high-speed Internet access, computer work stations, working design areas and tools, easily replicable supply stations, displays and publishing centers plus resources including artifacts, a research and reference library, and the list goes on.

The Academy is located in the heart of the historic and charming village of Comfort, Texas, in the beautiful Texas Hill country, 45 minutes from San Antonio and 1½ hours from Austin. Most convenient airport is San Antonio. Antiquing, shopping, golfing, fishing, bicycling, sightseeing, caving, natural and historic-site adventuring are popular area pursuits. Or just relaxing on the porch of your B&B!

Testimonial: "*I just returned from the Dinah Zike Academy, and I'm overwhelmed with the vast amount of information provided. This is my 37th year in education, and I've never enjoyed a course of study as much as the Academy.*"

For More Information, or to reserve your spot:

WEBSITE: www.dzacademy.com
PHONE: 830-995-3800
FAX: 830-995-3713   MAIL:
MAIL inquiries to:
DZ Academy, P. O. Box 340, Comfort TX 78013